The Gift

The Gift

A Glimpse Through the Window of My Soul

Elleen E. Ellis

XULON PRESS

Xulon Press
2301 Lucien Way #415
Maitland, FL 32751
407.339.4217
www.xulonpress.com

Paperback ISBN-13: 978-1-66284-969-5
Ebook ISBN-13: 978-1-66284-970-1

Acknowledgments

I have always written down my thoughts and feelings, since they could not be voiced without incurring a rebuke.

The ability to pour myself out after something happened not only to me but also to my family, friends, and the world, fascinated and intrigued me. Writing has always been therapeutic and cleansing, which helped me to make sense of some situations and find peace through others. This love for poetry has been a solace through many stormy and turbulent seasons of my life.

A special thanks goes to Valari King, who, after learning of my writing and subsequent unwillingness to publish for fear of baring my innermost thoughts, became my conscience and constant foot on my rear end to publish. I was apprehensive to have such a personal account exposed to the brunt of scrutiny and criticism, Thanks for not letting up, Sis.

This work has evolved from poetry to The Gift. It is a gift to share one's self with others and to leave an offering. I want to encourage anyone who is a poet or writer of any form who desires to share their work to just do it. There will always be critics among us, but that is how we learn and grow. There will be others who will disagree with the best of advice but remember, we give gifts with all our hearts and it is up to the recipient to appreciate the intent of the gift.

Enjoy unwrapping The Gift.

Blessings,

Elleen

Dedication

I dedicate this work of my soul to all kindred spirits who find solace and insight in poetry.

~~~~~~~~~~~~~~~

Photo credit: Al Frazier

Personally, I dedicate this book to Phil, the musical poet who resides in my heart. I love you deeply.

E. E. E.

Table of Contents

Part 3: The Gift of Healing and Letting Go of the Past

Part 4: The Gift of Blessings

Part 5: The Gift of Provision

Part 1
The Gift of Hope

Photo credit: D.E.E

The wound cannot heal unless you stop picking at the scab.

The Builders

Just yesterday
We lurched
From the precipices,
Exerted our strength,
Exploited our abilities.
Determined,
Yet so isolated.
Efficient,
Yet temporarily in crisis.
Just yesterday,
Deliberately,
We gained access.
Investing
In the ingenuity
Of their diligence and
And integrity
Their complexities.
Just yesterday
Revealed
Their resolve,
Undertook the enormity
Although valid and dedicated.
Just yesterday,
The district collaborations
Blended to merge

Innovations and trends.
Just yesterday,
Standing
Tall,
Domineering in opulence.
Today…destroyed infrastructures.

Unwrapping the Gift

Strength for Today

Why are you cast down, O my soul, and why are you in turmoil within me? Hope in God; for I shall again praise him, my salvation and my God.

~ Psalm 42:11

It's amazing how far I have come. I remember vividly as I and my friends would run barefooted and aimlessly without a care, playing and enjoying our childhood. I'm a long way from Sierra Leone, Freetown, where my roots are. This is a country that grips my heart in a deep, enduring embrace that is laced with passion and intimacy.

Can you imagine how far you have come from your roots? Maybe it's the other side of the town that no one wanted to be associated with. Maybe you come from a background filled with privileges some of us can only dream of. It is not the same for everyone, but one thing we share in common is that we all are not where we used to be. Some of us have moved forward and others have regressed.

I am far removed from that barefooted, carefree child I was back then, even though walking barefooted is natural and the most comfortable position for my feet.

I still walk barefooted.

Wherever you are in your station in life, the goal is not to stand still or regress, but to move forward and make progress. If you are not satisfied in your current situation, then do something about it. There is a lot that can be done—counseling helps. Pray and get some professional help and keep on praying, and then pray some more. Talk to your pastor or a trusted person, and keep on praying and trusting God to supply your needs. If financially you are strapped, pray as you cut off all the frivolous things and start living within your means. Pray that you stay faithful and consistent. Pray and keep on praying.

At the end of your days, you want to ensure that the dash between birth and death signifies a time well spent on this earth. If you are struggling, you must take a step back and take stock of yourself. What needs to change? Do you need to change something? Talk to the Lord about it. Pray. Then get ready to take the first step and do what it will take to restore your restless spirit. It is not going to be easy; nothing worth fighting for or living for is ever easy.

My gift to you: You can make it; just take it one day at a time, placing one foot in front of the other and keep moving forward. Pray!

That, my friend, is your gift for today.

Scar Tissue

Memories of a cut
Slashed across my abdomen long ago.
Fast-forward to a few weeks ago
I lay flat on a cold bed,
More slashes, inches apart
Same abdomen, same cold bed.
This time,
Scar tissue
Blocks the knife,
A blessing in disguise.
I breathe uneasily,
Trying to calm my fears,
Confused by thoughts of incompletion.
Scar tissue blessings?
I'm not sure.
But scar tissue
Saves the day.

Unwrapping the Gift

Strength for Today

"But I will restore you to health and heal your wounds," declares the Lord.

~ Jeremiah 30:17

No matter how minor the surgery, be it hand, urological, or as serious as neurosurgery, surgery is never entered into with nonchalance. As the date of my surgery drew near, I remained outwardly calm. Inside of me there was a churning river of emotion and fear. This was to be a "routine" surgery, as the doctor put it, in and out, but inwardly I was afraid because my mother had routine surgery and she had died.

Today is the day of my surgery, and I am very pensive and taking deep breaths to calm my heart. I am having thoughts of my mother and how calm she appeared on the day of her surgery. I have flashbacks of how I encouraged her and told her that we would see her later and that she would be just fine. I started saying the same words of encouragement to myself, but I also kept the past vivid and center stage in my thoughts.

We arrived at the hospital and checked in, and soon enough the doctor came in, accompanied by a lovely woman he introduced as his wife. She was off that day and, wanting to spend time with her husband, she decided to join him in operating on me together, which they explained they sometimes do when both had the day off. I told her I was glad she was to be a part of my medical team. Little did I know that she was the divine intervention at work on my behalf that day.

I awakened to my husband's soothing and gentle rub on my arm. He asked how I was feeling, if I was in any pain, and if I was alert. I replied, "Yes." I asked him what the doctor said. He explained that as the doctor began the surgery laparoscopically, his wife observed seeing something out of the ordinary. After a closer look, they determined that I had major scar tissue from other surgeries that had created a bond on some organs and the procedure could not continue as planned. My surgeon simply patched me up and withdrew the instruments and closed me up. I would need to have some other procedures to ensure my body was ready before completing the initial surgery.

I shook my head in disbelief. What? I'm in pain and there has to be a do-over? Then relief flooded my body; scar tissue had saved the day!

I suddenly realized that my past had saved me from a future I would not have liked if the surgery had continued without the observation of the scar tissue buildup. No one can move forward effectively while still carrying the burden of their past. Sometimes the past involves a fear of what-if. Moving forward is facing forward, with not only your body, but your mind by relinquishing everything that will keep you from getting to your goal. The past does not hold onto us; we hold onto it. If it is past, why not let it go? Do you realize that conjuring the past is like carrying a dead animal on your back? Soon it will start to decay, and then everyone around you will start smelling it, and then people will avoid you because when they come around, they smell the dead animal you've refused to bury or throw in the trash can.

Sometimes we hold on because we do not know how we will survive if we let go of what we think makes us relevant to society and our world. People will listen to me because I have a platform to talk about and to help others. Are you helping yourself though? Each time you share your story, does it bring back the painful past or is it therapeutic and cathartic for your soul? Only you can answer that question, my friend.

"How do I do that?" you ask. You never know how your situation and your life will change when you ask God to use you as you heal through the storms you have experienced. Maybe you are in a painful situation and you cannot see the blessings in your position. God is allowing you to gain experience so you can bless others with your story and witness.

I am thankful for that day because if it were not for the scar tissue that caused the doctor to stop, I would have been in a terrible state if the surgery had proceeded. We must be thankful for the experiences we are going through and have gone through.

My gift to you: Do you have scar tissue? Do you have scars left over from your past and the pain they left? You need to stop picking at the scabs of your scars so that the wound can heal. Healing will occur from the inside out; but stop picking at the scab. The past does not hold onto us, we hold onto the past. If it is P-A-S-T, why not let it go? Relinquish your past so you can breathe and live. You cannot move forward effectively while still carrying the burden of your past.

That, my friend, is your gift for today.

The Battle

The bed beckoned me.
Recline in my softness!
Reason scolded that I had
Many chores before I could rest.
My heart was undecided
In the decision to make.
Who would win this battle of the wills?
Stumbling over my well-worn slippers,
They groaned as I kicked them
Under the bed.
The warm covers smiled
As I slid quietly between the soft sheets.

Unwrapping the Gift

Strength for Today

And you will feel secure, because there is hope; you will look around and take your rest in security.

~ Job 11:18

I did not want to get out of bed; after all, it was Saturday, and apart from my chores, I did not have anywhere to go. My African upbringing chiseled away at my reasoning as I was reminded of my grandmother's words: "A woman who stays in bed till dawn is a lazy woman." Why can't I just be still and enjoy the comfort of my cozy bed if I want to? So many times we have been told things that still govern our lives. Yes, some of the old wives' tales our mothers, grandmothers, and family have told us were great sayings, but we have to treasure what works and let go of the others that do not enhance our lives.

Whether you are a woman or a man, you must not feel guilty about resting. So many times, our children and family pull us in so many directions and when we stop for even a moment, we feel that we are like the ever-moving Energizer Bunny running on Duracell batteries. Even batteries, no matter how strong and powerful, will give out sooner or later.

Have tradition and customs held you back? Now, I will never trade my upbringing and how it has helped to shape me into the woman I am today. Sometimes the body needs to rest, and today is that day. Chores can wait while your body rejuvenates. Stop feeling guilty because you spent an extra hour in bed. Many times, we are too hard on ourselves.

My gift to you: A body that is not rested is a body that is destined to break. I give you permission to put your feet up and enjoy the feeling of being still. Let your mind wander into blissful nothingness and relax. Rest—you will feel better. Self-care is the greatest testimony of appreciation for the body that God has given us.

That, my friend, is your gift for today.

Our Sons: From Boys to Men

We have to teach our sons how to become men;
That lesson transcends the definition
Of who and what a man is.
We allow our sons to watch violence
Both at home and on the streets.
They adopt heroes that are thugs.
We fail to teach them,
Showing them better examples,
Teaching them that their pants
Belong on their waist
Tightly fastened with a belt with their shirttails
tucked in.
We have to teach our sons,
Not forgetting the number one lesson;
Teaching by our own example,
Which we can only pray
They somehow emulate.
That lesson should extend
To the way they carry themselves;
Head held high,
Pride in who they are as a person
With the right to breathe this God-given air.
To step out into the world
With confidence
That speaks of their inner greatness.

We must teach our sons
How to be courteous and respectful,
How to stand firm in their beliefs,
But also teach them how to back down,
Especially when they cannot support their arguments
And when the opponent begins to show physical
aggression.
We must teach them the most important lesson:
It takes more than their fists to become a man.
It's a complete package.
We must teach our sons
That being a man is not about making babies;
Certainly not about carrying a gun.
Being a man involves the ability
To know their own minds,
Getting a useful education
To support themselves and their family.
Teaching our sons that
The reputation they create
May one day be the deciding factor
In a court of law.
Teaching our sons to become men
Is to teach them that the B-word
is a derogatory term.
It does not signify endearment,
Nor is it
The first or middle name of every female
Who angers them
But that using it
Signifies their own
Lack of self-worth.

Teaching our sons to be men
Is one of the most challenging tasks given to parents.
However, the charge is also ours;
We take up the mantle.
We show our sons
How we lean on God to be our guide.
We show our sons
How we cry out to our Heavenly Father
For our every need, which he does supply.
We show our sons
How to respect their mothers and sisters
By how we relate to our women and daughters.
By our own actions
We teach our sons;
Each day we live
We are teaching our sons
To be the man that we are!

Unwrapping the Gift

Strength for Today

Be strong and courageous. Do not fear or be in dread of them, for it is the Lord your God who goes with you. He will not leave you or forsake you.

~ Deuteronomy 31:6

As I wrote that piece, I was deeply affected by the turmoil the parents of Trayvon Martin endured. They had to delay their grief for their son, who had been killed; they had to hold back their sorrow as a family as they faced media scrutiny of who they are as parents, the character of their son, and they had to face all of this daily with shoulders back and heads held up high.

I do not personally know the parents, but I have enough empathy to feel their immense pain through my television screen. My heart ached for them. I felt tears cascade down my face along with the pain that was etched on their faces. I wept with them.

As parents of a son, in this day and age, we have to educate our children on how to face fears and when to back down. Turning away from trouble is not a sign of weakness but a sign of discernment. Our sons are endangered species, and we must educate and show them how to walk this earth.

I am angered at the thought that parents even have to differentiate between skin tones and police brutality. It's comparable to negligence if parents don't connect with their sons about what it means to be a Black man and how to carry oneself in a world that is determined to misunderstand and malign them.

My mother used to explain to us when we complained that our parents were too harsh that parents are not raising children to be good citizens at home because they will be good at home since discipline is applied to negative behaviors. She said that children are guided on how to behave outside the home because the streets will not be loving and kind to them, so they need to learn at home how to behave when they step outside the home.

My gift to you: This is a cruel and unjust world. The wealthy and strong continue to prey on the poor and the weak, and its unfairness brings to mind that one day, justice cannot help but prevail. We cannot stand idly by as our children are gunned down and crucified for being in the skin that God encased them in. Be proud of who you are because you are indeed uniquely and wonderfully made. Let's teach our children not only to be proud of their uniqueness but to preserve their uniqueness. Let's teach our children to choose which causes to fight for, the ones to walk away from, which to pray about, and the ones to join in solidarity and support.

That, my friend, is your gift for today.

My Eyes Are Watching

I watch them each day
As they struggle to juggle
The expectations,
Responsibilities,
And engagements.
These young minds:
Ingenious
Defining
Accomplished
Exploited
Undertaking great responsibilities.
These young minds,
I watch them each day
As they struggle to juggle
The battles that rage
Underneath the surface.
These young minds:
Identifying
Investing
Preparing
Determined
Surrendering.
I watch them each day
As they struggle to juggle
Who they are,

The expectations,
The pressures.
These young minds,
I watch them each day, and
Each day they remold themselves.

Unwrapping the Gift

Strength for Today

For everything there is a season, and a time for every matter under heaven:

~ Ecclesiastes 3:1

I have been a part of the public school system in America for the past twenty-one years. Each day, I interact with students and see their struggles to make sense of who they are and the expectations of the standards they are being taught. I know I encourage my students to excel to higher heights that exceed their imaginations as I create innovative lessons to help stimulate and motivate them to crave success.

As I teach, I am constantly changing my methods to customize to student needs. A one-day lesson could be expanded over two days to ensure that my students grasp the concepts, and sometimes even when I have to move on to another topic, the previous one is revised and revisited so that students can eventually get it.

A long time ago, I taught pottery and the students would get an unshaped mound of clay and begin to fashion it into the desired piece. At the end of each class period, the work in progress would be covered up with a wet cloth and a plastic bag fastened securely over the piece to keep it from drying up.

That process reminds me of ourselves. We need to chisel away at the undesirable situations and things in our lives a little at a time till we get the desired effect. It is doable if you set your mind to it.

What are you struggling with? Does your life need to be restructured? Are you trying to change too many things at once? Start with one thing, one goal at a time, and then move on to the next project. You will feel a sense of accomplishment instead of the depressing sense of failure because of a full basket of goals to accomplish all at once. This is like me in my classroom. Take a step back to analyze your immediate needs and attend to those first and then tackle the others one task at a time.

My gift to you: You are not a stone, immovable and unmalleable. We all can change and adjust to situations. We all have the ability to improve and to make changes for the better. Don't stand still, planted in the ground—you are not a tree. Move and grow and improve, and when you improve and make positive changes in your life, they will translate into other areas of your life as well. You can remold your life one task at a time so that the clay of your life does not dry up.

That, my friend, is your gift for today.

Lose To Win

Failures
Struggles
I just can't seem to get it right.
Third loss
Two years in a row
Giving too much of me seems to be my downfall.
A bit here
A bit there?
How can I give some and not all?
It's either all of me or none of me!
Is that what it takes to have a lasting relationship?
Not really committing to anyone
Holding back the vulnerabilities?
Giving all is a sign.
Total commitment.
Sometimes we have to lose ourselves
To gain something better than what we had before.

Unwrapping the Gift

Strength for Today

The LORD is close to the brokenhearted and saves those who are crushed in spirit.

~ Psalm 34:18

Have you ever lost in a situation and yet felt like you won? Looking at the title of the poem, it seems a bit ridiculous. I lose so I can win? When I lose, I feel like the word defines me: loser. In the words of this poem, I had a great loss. I lost a friendship I treasured and it hurt so much, just thinking of it made it hard for me to breathe.

Through this loss, I was able to see aspects of the relationship that I had not allowed myself to see before the separation. Two people I thought would be by my side left me at the time I needed them most. Through those losses, I have gained so much more. Great as they were, I now have a joy and peace that I never had before with those individuals in my life. I never realized those relationships were not healthy.

I reassessed my life and cleaned up my emotional stockroom. I found a peace I did not know was lacking. My family came to my rescue. They rallied around me and embraced me and loved me through the hurt and pain.

With this newfound peace, I can claim victory in my loss. I lost friendships that I treasured, but I have become a winner of the ultimate gift: peace of mind. Some relationships are not healthy when you are the only one giving. People will take and take until they suck you dry. When you are in the relationship, you can feel the blood leaving your body until they suddenly let go. Then you realize that you are almost out of your air and blood supply.

My gift to you: Count yourself a winner when you suffer such losses. It's time to pick yourself up and get on with life. Live your most fulfilling life and enjoy your newfound freedom. Never forget: Do not replace the blood-sucking, emotionally draining relationships with new ones.

Learn from the former and enter a level playing field of friendships where there is give and take, and it is not so draining.

That, my friend, is your gift for today.

The Empty House

What depressing sadness
Overwhelming and hollow
Emptiness inside.
No love
No care
Empty as an abandoned house.
Emotions long gone
Ripped out
Castrated
Destroyed from the inside out.
What sadness
Alive
Yet dead
Emotionally strangled
You low-grade thief.
I trusted you
But you pilfered
Plundered
Damaged and destroyed.
Breathless, unbelievable
Sycophant
Lowest of beings
Stole the intangible.
Left alone and afraid
Empty as an abandoned house
One day, you will meet your end.

Unwrapping the Gift

Strength for Today

But blessed is the one who trusts in the Lord, whose confidence is in him. They will be like a tree planted by the water that sends out its roots by the stream. It does not fear when heat comes; its leaves are always green. It has no worries in a year of drought and never fails to bear fruit.

~ Jeremiah 17:7–8

I had introduced poetry to my reading class as a literary text and at the culmination of the class, I asked them to write freestyle poetry. As most teachers do, I brought the poetry home to read over the weekend. A very bright student, new to my class, had written a poem describing her body as an empty house. She described the horrors of feeling like an empty shell. She felt unloved and unwanted through the words of her poem. Needless to say, I was concerned after reading the poem because it sounded so defeated, but I was more concerned because I needed to make sure this student was all right emotionally and physically.

The next day was Monday, and I made sure to alert our SAFE coordinator of the poem and later to chat with the student to make sure they were all right. I was relieved to know the student would be alright and sad to discover the family moved a lot as the single mother tried to find normalcy for her family.

Sometimes we too might feel like an empty house. We feel we do not have control over our lives and that we do not matter in the grand scheme of occurrences over our lives. What have you been ripped of? We are ripped of our dreams when we allow our fears to overtake us. Have you ripped someone of his or her dreams? We do it to our children, telling them they will amount to nothing. We do it to our friends, giving them bad advice. We do it to ourselves when we refuse to move forward and take chances, like starting a business, or returning to or completing our education. We rid ourselves of blessings when we do not use the talents God has blessed us with.

My gift to you: Take courage, my friend. Pray for strength and don't just sit there, move on! You have your blessings, so reach out and claim them. If you don't stretch out your hand, you won't receive what is right there for you. Take it! You matter!

That, my friend, is your gift for today.

The Return

So excited about returning.
The awakening
Time to rediscover
To explore.
So excited to return
The sights,
Smells to associate and differentiate
The difference from then to now.
So excited to return the buildings
Unique infrastructure,
This way of life
Of my people.
So excited to return.
Sounds of the morning
Calls from loud speakers,
Prayer criers on the streets.
So excited to return
Calls for the faithful,
Hurrying feet of children
Clanging of pots and pails
Children jostling at the pump.
So excited to return
Harsh, firm cries.
"Make haste with that water!"
Cleansing of the body

Final blares from above and the street
White, ethereal domes resounding.
So excited to return.
Dawn is breaking.
The day officially has begun.
These are the sounds of home.
So excited to return;
I'm home.

Unwrapping the Gift

Strength for Today

Brothers, I do not consider that I have made it my own. But one thing I do: forgetting what lies behind and straining forward to what lies ahead.

~ Philippians 3:13

I left Sierra Leone in April 1996. I was reluctant to leave the place of my birth and go to a place that was strange, even when rumors told me that it promised opportunity and wealth. There were close to four million people who would gladly trade places with me.

Fast-forward to June 2013. I am returning to Sierra Leone—my birthplace—after seventeen years. As the plane approaches Lungi Airport and I begin to see the lush trees, houses of various sizes and colors, and people appearing, I am filled with an overwhelming sadness. Why has it taken me so long to want to return to my ancestral home, this land that I love? I keep asking myself this question as we touch down on the tarmac, and I am jolted back to reality. I am home!

What are your regrets? What have you put off doing? Is it a book you never read, a trip you never took, a place you want to see, a call you need to make, someone you need to talk to, someone you need to tell that you are sorry, a decision you need to make? You can choose to live on top of the fence called regret or you can jump off the fence and stop saying "I wish I could do this or I wish things were different." Tell yourself you are ready to move forward, cautiously, but with one foot in front of the other. Move away from Regret Ville and towards the future.

My gift to you: Today, I challenge you to move forward to do one thing that may cause you to sleep better tonight. One thing will lead to another. Move forward!

That, my friend, is your gift for today.

Change

Many times
I try to hide,
Thinking of my pride,
Seeing how other minds
Try to make me whine.
But
I am resolved
In helping myself
With the guidance of God to
Evolve.
There will be a total
Dissolve
Of those
Who try to make me cry.
So I'm taking my stride
To the other side
Of the divide.
Change has come
It is here to stay.
Change is here;
Embrace it.
Lay the pride aside
Accept it
Embrace it
Receive it.

Unwrapping the Gift

Strength for Today

"For I know the plans I have for you," declares the LORD, "plans to prosper you and not to harm you, plans to give you hope and a future."

~ Jeremiah 29:11

Change means to be different from what you were before. Change is deliberately deciding to do only that which will serve your highest good and a decision is made to do something different. Change is difficult to commit to and to maintain.

To change from what you were to a new form leaves a lot to accomplish.

Change is one of the most difficult things I have had to endure. I am a very structured person, and the structure is in place for me to survive and cope. When I am forced to change, I am unsettled, and there is a great period of self-talk. I now have to look at and analyze the many parts of the change to see things from another's perspective. When doing this, I synthesize their reasoning into how it will fit within my structure and even how I can move things around in my well-ordered life to do the new thing. I have to convince myself that change will be for the better. This is not natural and does not settle well with me.

We are not always right. "This is the way we've always done things," does not mean it is the right way to move forward. The way things are ordered in our lives is not necessarily the best. Look at yourself as a lifelong learner, and you will begin to see that growth is good. We are not talking about chin hairs; we are talking about improvement in your life to make things better for you, whether it is on a personal or professional level. Change could be good.

My gift to you: You can change. If you want to make a change in your life, you are capable of making that change. It will be hard, but it is doable. There is hope if you accept, receive, and allow God to lead and guide you. None of us are unredeemable. Claim what is yours and take your rightful place. You will feel better, and you will fulfill your purpose when you allow yourself to change. Do not close the window to change. Look at it; leave your emotions out of the decision because change is uncomfortable but necessary if you are to grow. Try change, and keep an open mind to the possibilities. If it does not work out quite the perfect way you had hoped and you have given your best effort, you can be satisfied because you tried.

That, my friend, is your gift for today.

Leaving

Leaving reminds me of a death,
Eternally taken away
To be reunited at the Rapture.
Answers elude me
As I question
Why now?
Verifying the facts,
We have no abiding city here.
Interestingly enough,
Our frail bodies
Will one day
Succumb to death's call,
Sometimes unwelcomed.
Naturally,
We miss all those gone on before;
Gone to wait,
To be
Our great cloud of witnesses.
Leaving
Is actually
Going.
Going to prepare—
For me.

Unwrapping the Gift

Strength for Today

But, as it is written, "What no eye has seen, nor ear heard, nor the heart of man imagined, what God has prepared for those who love him."

~ 1 Corinthians 2:9

I keep remembering the first time I heard someone say, "We have to live each day as if it were our last day on earth." So many times, we live as if we will live forever on this earth. We won't! I think we tend to have a God complex with ourselves and because our bodies are strong and we are beautiful with youth and vitality, we think we will never get sick or grow old and eventually die.

What does it mean to live life as if each day was our last? We should live life with intention. That means we are living life with purpose and living life deliberately. Each day, we have a choice to be kind, to love, to eat healthier, to exercise, to start that business, to leave a toxic relationship and stay away from toxic persons, and to keep putting our best foot forward.

There is hope. When we are Christian, our faith reassures us of eternal life after death. That is why we believe that this right here is temporal and that even though our earthly bodies will break and all things fall apart, there is a place prepared for us by the Father. There, we will not endure any more suffering or strife. We will live forever in Heaven, praising and rejoicing with a host of others singing praises to our Lord and Savior.

My gift to you: We will all die one day. There is good news, though: We will live forever. We either will live in an eternity of torment in a sulfuric fire, bound and gnashing our teeth, or praising God with other heavenly hosts, wearing golden robes and crowns, living in mansions prepared specifically for us, and experiencing everlasting peace forevermore. Live intentionally with eternity in mind because the rewards of a heavenly eternity and peace are our rewards for endurance.

That, my friend, is your gift for today.

Part 2
The Gift of Love

Photo credit: D.E.E

When you gaze at me, I feel warmth, even in the cold. Your gentlest touch causes my heart to flutter, even after all these years. I know, for sure, this is love.

The One

How do you know
That he is the one for you?
How can you tell
He is the one
You can finally trust your heart to?
How do you know you can now let go of
The emotions you've kept at bay,
To finally share
Something of yourself to another?
When can you tell
He is here
In your life to stay?
When can you finally realize
He is the one
Who has been sent your way?
When do you realize
After all these years of
Futile searching,
Waiting,
That this one was created
Just for you?
When will you trust?
Finally open your eyes,
Forgetting the past
To see that this one

Is the one?

Unwrapping the Gift

Strength for Today

And let us not grow weary of doing good, for in due season we will reap, if we do not give up.

~ Galatians 6:9

How can I know "the one" who was born to be my life mate? This is the second-most important decision a person can make in their life.

Everyone wants someone to call their own. Not everyone will be fortunate to find someone of the opposite sex who will become a friend, confidante, and life partner: that one person who will share life's sorrows and joys – the person who will be an encourager and support when the other wants to pursue dreams and goals that will benefit the union.

Sometimes we are in too much of a hurry to be married or "settled," and we do not take time to study and understand a person we want to share our lives with. We tend to forget that this handsome or beautiful person was raised by parents other than ours, has had life experiences different than ours, and sometimes is of a different culture than our own. Entering a covenant with the purpose to love, cherish, honor, and respect the other is not one to enter into lightly, but so many do, with horrifying results.

Some of us are bogged down with the cares of the past and we cannot break free of the memories of what some other person did to us. I am not going to attempt to fix your past. It has to be left there with other things that have occurred so you can now enjoy what you have with this significant person. If you need counseling to heal, then that is what you must do—as long as you remember that you owe it to your significant other to be the very best version of yourself. You promised and gave your word, so you must keep your word.

My gift to you: There is that one person who God has for you. So many times, we choose for ourselves and then when things do not go right, we use the blame game and want to put the blame on someone other than ourselves. Allow God to show you the one for you, and trust his process. The answer will be clear. If the one is the one, you will not have to jump through hoops because God will clear the path and make it plain that this is the chosen person for you. Stop looking over your shoulder at what that other person did to you and looking to see if your partner will repeat the same.

That, my friend, is your gift for today.

I Got Exactly What I Needed

I always told myself
I would know him
When I see him.
Little did I know
What I thought I knew
Was just a little girl's dream,
A fantasy.
I always told myself
He would be as tall as Freetown's Cotton Tree
Dark as the ebony Bondo mask
Skin as smooth as the Nomoli
Lips as red as the African setting sun
Eyes liquid gold and deep
As the rivers flowing around the peninsula.
Hands as strong as the grasp of a chimpanzee.
I always told myself
He would love family,
He does.
He would love God above all else,
He does.
He would support me in all my endeavors,
He surely does.
He would partner with me
To create a home for me
And our children,

He did.
He would be a man after God's own heart,
A man I could look on and be proud of.
He surely is.
I told myself many things
When I was a little girl.
And now,
As I look up into your caramel eyes,
Your skin as light as honey,
Lips sensual and full
Hands as gentle and contrastingly firm,
Eyes that speak volumes in depth,
You look into my very soul,
Can read and understand
When words are needless.
I take a hold of your strong arms
As I bow in gratitude
To the Heavenly Father.
He did not give me what the little girl dreamt of;
He gave me exactly what I needed.

Unwrapping the Gift

Strength for Today

For everything God created is good, and nothing is to be rejected if it is received with thanksgiving, because it is consecrated by the word of God and prayer.

~ 1 Timothy 4:4-5

Have you ever told yourself with satisfaction that you have exactly what you need? We want a successful career, money, clothes, shoes, a man, a woman, a house, children, great health a long life, and of course, the list goes on.

As a child, I often dreamed of what my man would look like. I figured he would be dark and commanding, like my father and my African heroes. Little did I know that he wouldn't even be born on my continent! God had what I needed across the Atlantic. The man God had for me was born into a family as diverse from my heritage as the east is to the west.

What notions do you hold about your future? Have you already decided your future? If that is the case, then you must know that in your future awaits problems of great magnitude because you might want what you desire, but that is not what God wants for you. It is not part of his plan for you if you are a Christian.

I did not get what I wanted, but I got what I needed: a man gentle enough to soothe my explosive personality, a man strong enough to calm my spirit with a smothering glance, a man who loves God which exudes from him into our home. He is a man I trust with my emotions, my dreams, my goals, and who is secure enough to support me through it all. He is a man whose skin is as light as caramel and shades of the African setting sun. He is a man I am proud to call my very own with no reservation. He is a quiet man, and a man of honor, integrity and dignity.

Give thanks for the loved ones in your life. We do not get what we need because for some of us, we are not thankful for what we have already been given. God does not bless an ungrateful person.

That, my friend, is your gift for today.

Fooled

I can't believe I allowed this
Again.
I thought I was smarter.
You crept in
Unexpectedly,
Scrambling over my roadblocks;
Blocks of caution;
Roadblocks of suspicion and doubt.
Your packaging was attractive;
Smooth talker,
Golden-tongued salesman.
The past was laid to rest,
Forgotten like old wives' tales.
Big mistake!
I should have tread lightly,
Cautiously,
Never forgetting the days of old.
I should have let you in ever so slowly,
But I was both gullible
And even stupid.
I should have never forgot
When smooth words,
Deceitful words,
Like pebbles in a running brook
Allowed me to swing wide

The gates of my heart
Rusted with age,
Creaked wide
To allow your sweetness
Filling me now but reverting to ashes.
I can't believe I allowed this;
I, who thought
I was smart.
You crept in unexpectedly,
Callous you,
Embezzler of hearts!
Next time,
I will be wiser.
Ready.

Unwrapping the Gift

Strength for Today

Be kind to one another, tenderhearted, forgiving one another, as God in Christ forgave you.

~ Ephesians 4:32

I grew up with a saying: The first time you are made a fool of does not make you a fool. But the second time you allow the same situation, then you are a fool.

I've always thought myself a fairly smart person. I always use my intuition, which allows me to read and study people in a way I think no one else can. Then I was slapped upside the head by the unexpected. A person I loved and had pegged as trustworthy had smoothly slipped through my savviness and my defenses and entered my heart. When this friend let me down, I did not only feel hurt, I felt shame. I was ashamed because I had allowed this person into my family, and I had even said some hard words to some of my family members in defense of this person.

I had been warned, but I categorized the warning as a sign of jealously. Inside, I thought my family was jealous so I gave them deaf ears.

When I got hurt, I didn't know how to explain it to my family and to other friends and for a long time, I pretended that all was well; but inside, I died a little bit each day.

For a long time, I couldn't bring myself to tell them. Then one day, I called each of my family members to tell them what had occurred and one of my sisters said, "I am sorry that your relationship ended this way. However, life goes on. It's better to be in peace than to deal with the drama of the situation. I am sure [the other person] will regret it one day. Let's pray for [that person], because I am sure they are hurting too."

What? This person hurt me and I should pray for them? It took a while to realize that they too must feel hurt, and so I began to add the person to my prayer list and slowly, as God healed my heart, I honestly asked that God heal them too. I am not saying this to trivialize the situation, but I can tell you, this process took me a couple of years to release the hurt, betrayal, and brokenness.

My gift to you: When we feel fooled, betrayed, and let down, let's never forget that we are not alone. So as we pray for healing, let's also lift the other person up to be restored by God. It is not easy to forgive, but we forgive not for them, but to get the monkey off our backs. Remember, the only person who we never want to withdraw their love from us is the One who created us, and God will never leave nor forsake us.

That, my friend, is your gift for today.

We See Them

We see them
Huddled
Deep in thought
Contemplating
Complicated
Muddled thoughts.
We see them
Undertake the test
That determines,
Defines, and verifies
Their abilities
To progress to the next stage.
We see them
Reveal their resolve,
Tenacity,
Each one isolated,
Deeply concentrating,
Distinctly engaged,
Contemplating the task.
We see them,
Diligent, engaged,
Prepared, reflective,
Exerting,
Validating
Their very essence.

We see them,
Excelling and eager,
Efficient.
We see them ready
To take on life's challenges.
We see them
And we watch them succeed.

Unwrapping the Gift

Strength for Today

*But if you do not forgive others their trespasses,
neither will your Father forgive your trespasses.*

~ Matthew 6:15

It is amazing how we walk through streets, drive by, and fail to see our surroundings. As a high school teacher, sometimes I drive to other schools and after getting to my destination, I wonder how I even got there because I was not aware of my surroundings.

We do the same to people sometimes. We see them, but we do not see them. No one wants to be a nobody in someone's mind. People matter, and when we acknowledge the people we pass by, they are realizing their personal place in this world.

It is important to remind ourselves that if we want to matter to others, we have to acknowledge the people around us also. Most days when I get to work, I usually do not encounter anyone because I am there earlier than my coworkers. But every now and then I will meet others in our staff lounge and greet them; it's amazing how often I have to repeat myself because they are so used to others coming in and not acknowledging their presence! Sometimes I repeat my greeting with a bite to my tone because I find it disrespectful to greet and not get a response.

My gift to you: Take time today to nod and acknowledge people as you pass them by. Yes, I know making eye contact with some people means you may have something they possibly can swindle out of you. Acknowledgements come in various forms. Smile and let it reach your eyes so people actually feel your smile, and it will give warmth to them.

That, my friend, is your gift for today.

Submission

Contemplating
Deepest thoughts
Decisions looming
Wondering
If it is the best choice.
Thinking aloud and scared.
Meditating
Lord, please help me make it through.
Hear my prayer
Comfort my soul
Keep me close
As I lean heavily on you.
Yielding
Broken in spirit
Nothing else left to do
Bringing my crisis
The doubts and fears
Laying them all at your feet.
Surrender
Completely
Without agitation
Without anxiety
No longer threatened
By failure
By pestilence

Deeply rooted in the promise:
A divine love that reassures
All is made whole in his will.
Blessed assurance
I contemplate and meditate,
Yielded
Total surrender
To the will
Of the Master Planner.

Unwrapping the Gift

Strength for Today

As the mountains surround Jerusalem, so the Lord surrounds His people from this time forth and forever.

~ Psalm 125:2

What do you mean I have to submit? To give up my rights to someone else? No way! So many of us have an issue with the word submission and think that being submissive means allowing someone else to control you. Many of us think that to submit is to allow another person to take control of our lives. Why is it so difficult to let go of our control? Yes, that's just what it is…control.

We have all surely seen senseless car accidents at inter-sections simply because someone did not want to submit the way of right to another person, even when they knew it was not their turn to go through. We have seen marriages fail because of an unwillingness to submit to the other spouse, even at the expense of their marriage.

What, then, exactly is submission? It is an act of yielding to another. We want to be so much in control. Are we in control? Are we really in control of our lives? If you are honest with yourself, you know that you are not in control of anything. We give ourselves a false sense of security to make ourselves feel good. The ultimate submission is a total surrender to God.

I surrender to God because I believe that he alone is in control. He has the power to tell me that I am breathing my last breath today. He alone is in control, and as his child, I am entrusting him to guide my steps, and I yield to him to oversee my life.

My gift to you: Do you need to surrender today? Are you blocking your blessings because you do not want to submit to the Master Planner? How can he lead you if you do not submit and surrender to his authority? I can assure you of a peace that will come over you so great—but only if you let go of the rope. Most of us live a tug-of-war life. Remember the game where two teams tug on a rope to determine the stronger team that pulls the weaker team over a demarcating line? Let us not live that life. Tread cautiously with the world but trustingly with God, and fall into his loving arms. He is right there beside you. Relinquish the driver's seat to the Divine Master and he will navigate you through life. Just let go! Be blessed!

That, my friend, is your gift for today.

The Soul

Deep in the soul,
Embedded within
Sinew and tissue
Lies the reticent
Desire to break from the saturnine.
The mystical,
Plausible, and astute qualities
That require reason
The shrewd observation,
Understanding
Of the most recondite soul
Seemly calm
Outwardly,
Inwardly cowardice,
This soul seeks strength,
Healing…a balm.
Deep in this soul lies love.

Unwrapping the Gift

Strength for Today

But seek first the kingdom of God and his righteousness, and all these things will be added to you.

~ Matthew 6:33

When I was a child, I often wondered: What am I made of? Of course, I knew my body was comprised of bone, muscle, and tissue and such, but what really makes me, me? I would look at my eleven brothers and sisters and admire them for one reason or another and wondered about myself. I did not and could not see the person that I was becoming. I was just a kid who had older brothers and sisters who I just thought were so perfect in what I could see. I saw their strengths and wanted to be just like them.

I know you too may have wondered who you are. It takes a lifetime for many people to identify who they are. In fact, many people spend a lifetime trying to answer that question, just like I did, and the answer has been there all along.

In fact, who I am is a strong Christian woman, the disciplined teacher, the go-getter, the wife, the mother, the entrepreneur, the friend, the sister, the confidante. Who am I? The daughter of the Most High King is my favorite title. God's favorite child. I realize that although I may still question not who I am but what my purpose here is on this earth, I have also realized that purpose changes. It has surely changed over the years as the seasons of my life have changed. But the part that knows that I am not just a walking being but that I belong to and am accountable to the One who made me does not change.

Who are you? You are a child of the Most High and he has a purpose for you! Many others will try to define who you are, but you are a child of the King. The many hats we wear will define us but as we continue to live this life, our main purpose here is to live a life that reflects the light of the One who created us.

My gift to you: Live your best life, Child of God! If you move away and stray from the path God has purposed for you, the enemy will derail you. You win when you move forward, even though situations try to put you in your grave. Move on and stay strong.

That, my friend, is your gift for today.

Amazing Blessings

Ever loving,
Helping the needy.
Living a life
That is worthy of blessings
Flowing from above.
Uplifting souls for refreshing,
Promoting, and encouraging
Those who have lost
All hope in humanity.
Evaluating self,
Moving forward towards perfection,
Never faltering,
Always acknowledging
My own strength and
Weaknesses.
Coming back to the Father
Firmly and deeply rooted
In his very care;
My heart is blessed.

Unwrapping the Gift

Strength for Today

Therefore I tell you, whatever you ask in prayer, believe that you have received it, and it will be yours.

~ Mark 11:24

Open your heart and look deep within and start thanking God for all he has given you. Open your eyes to see the blessings of a new day, and give thanks you have eyes to see. Start being grateful for one thing, and each day, add another. Keep doing that and see how full your life will be and then watch as God's Spirit will overflow in your life.

I used to struggle when asking God for what I needed or wanted. Sometimes, I just wanted to wallow in self-pity because I thought I lacked what I wanted. I came to realize that God cares about my needs. He will give me my wants—sometimes—but it is my needs that are a top priority for God. I acknowledge that he is my Heavenly Father; I got what I asked for from God. I had prayed and told the Lord that he is my Father and he knows how to give the best gifts, so I am entrusting myself totally to him so he can pick out and give me my gift.

We often ask God for "things," but we tell him what we want. Why are you asking him then? We must learn to say, "Lord, you know what I need. Please choose the best that you have for me and give it to me."

My gift to you: Ask and you shall receive. We tend to ask God for our heart's desires and when we receive them, we move on like we earned all we have without the blessings of God. We must always be grateful for what we have been given, and we will get more. My mother would always say, "An ungrateful heart is a heart filled with sin." I know how I feel when someone shows their gratitude after I have done something good for them. Our Heavenly Father wants us to show our gratitude. Ask and believe and trust that God will fulfill your needs. Do not come to God with hands outstretched to receive when you have not thanked him for all he has already done for you. Ingratitude is when we fail to give thanks for all that we have, and that is a sin.

That, my friend, is your gift for today.

I Worship

My eyes flutter
Open.
You have awakened me
Again;
I see a new day.
I cannot comprehend
The fact that
You bless others also
With this same amazing, gentle touch,
This awakening touch,
Whispering get up and
Praise me.
Your presence everywhere,
Your awesomeness unexplained.
All I can do
At this very moment
Is bow my head
With a very contrite heart
In gratitude
For unmerited favor.
I worship.

Unwrapping the Gift

Strength for Today

Give thanks in all circumstances; for this is the will of God in Christ Jesus for you.

~ 1 Thessalonians 5:18

Have you ever wondered how God does it? I go to sleep, and sometimes my sleep is restless based on what is happening in my life. Many nights I toss and turn and fail to rest and give my cares to the Lord, and then many times between the hours of 4:00 a.m. and 5:00 a.m. I feel a gentle nudge and a soft breath of life caress my face whispering, "Wake up, my precious child. Rise and worship me. Give me all the honor and all the praise. Let others see my glory shine through you."

I treasure the early morning wake-up calls from my Heavenly Father. I spend time talking to him and listening to him talk to me through his Holy Word. There is a certain peace I have, and sometimes I feel like I am God's favorite child, since the early wake-up is so special to me.

My neighbor Mr. Cleveland often says, "We are not in charge of nothing." It is easy to say we trust God when all is well in our world. Do you trust God when your heart is shattered by the death of a loved one, loss of work, abandonment, and disappointment? That is where our faith blooms and shines. In the critical moments when we cannot see beyond our own noses is the best way to prove our total dependence on God.

My gift to you: Today, as you rest in your bed, thank God for his love and care for you during your day and then ask him to take care of you as you rest. Sleep, my dear friend, and give it all to him. When you wake up, you will be refreshed.

We have all seen the contented look on a baby's face cradled in the arms of their parents. Give yourself over and rest easy in his bosom so you can find peace forevermore.

That, my friend, is your gift for today.

His Love

Often, we doubt if God is here.
Frail humans need tangibles.
When we look closer
Through the eyes
Of our hearts
We see him shining through
Through his love.
Each time we doubt
He says,
My love is so deep
You cannot get under it;
My love is so wide
You cannot go around it;
My love is so high
You cannot possibly jump over it.
Child, my love is sufficient for you.
When trouble visits us
We forget it is not forever.
We fall apart
As if he is not holding our hand.
We often wonder
Why we even bother
To walk the narrow road.
In times of plenty,
We often fail to thank him.

We claim our successes
As badges of self-sufficiency.
We celebrate,
Take all the credit,
Forgetting that he has carried us
All the way through.

Unwrapping the Gift

Strength for Today

And without faith it is impossible to please him, for whoever would draw near to God must believe that he exists and that he rewards those who seek him.

~ Hebrews 11:6

I have always been that person who prefers actions to words. Show me you love me. Show me that you care. Show me you feel my pain. Show me that I am your friend. Show me. Show me. Show me. I show people how I feel about them, and I want reciprocal actions.

We cannot dictate how God shows us love. God's love is everywhere. We awaken to a new day…God loves us. We get up out of bed, can move on our own steam…God loves us. We use our wheel chairs or walker…God loves us. We get dressed, someone helps us get dressed, eat, get into our cars or walk to take a bus or someone picks us up…God loves us. We have a place to go and make our livelihoods…God loves us. We have people to call us Mom, Dad, family, friend…God loves us.

I have wondered if God is there when I have been in situations that I thought God should have swooped in to save me from whatever it is I'm enduring. I have also wondered if he really takes my feelings into consideration when he allows things to happen or when he makes his decisions considering my life. Life's trials have sucker-punched me and the thought has crossed my mind as I wonder if God cares for me when my pain runs deep and I am "in my feelings."

My gift to you: Everything you have around you is a blessing from God. That is how he shows us that he loves us. Even the beggar on the street has clothes on his back or someone to stop and give him a dollar. That is a blessing. When we begin to actually see our blessings and the treasures that so many would gladly exchange places with us for, then we will be secure in God's love. You can never experience the grace of God's love if all you see is what you don't have.

That, my friend, is your gift for today.

Friendship

I have come to the painful realization
That the ones who are closest to us
Will hurt us the most,
Those we allow into the inner circle
Who are privy to our private thoughts.
They get close when others only wish
They could exchange places with them.
These people we allow to get in, to get close,
They open the sealed doors:
Doors that have been sealed for decades.
They bring down barricaded gates
That have been reinforced after each
disappointment in life.
These people; we have become accustomed to
Become very comfortable with them.
They have warmed and thawed
Our frozen hearts.
We let our defenses down
In the wake of their overtures.
They open their arms,
We run to the warmth of their acceptance.
In our minds, we call it love,
That ideology that only exists
In a made-up world
Of deceit and what we want to believe in.

We have conjured in our own minds
This dream of idyllic people,
These make-believe people
Who seem so perfect for us.
We dare not breathe
Lest our illusion dissipate,
Vanishing into thin air
From our foolish, overactive brains.
This perfect world,
These self-created images
Of the ones we care for,
Those we take into our minds.
Now we must watch
As the façade we have constructed
For our own assurances
Stumbles and crumbles,
Falls and disintegrates,
Forever gone
To a graveyard called Reality,
A graveyard called The Past.
Rest in peace.
Rest.
Rest in perfect peace,
Friendship.

Unwrapping the Gift

Strength for Today

My little children, I am writing these things to you so that you may not sin. But if anyone does sin, we have an advocate with the Father, Jesus Christ the righteous.

~ 1 John 2:1

I had never known how to make friends. Everyone in my circle was family. As I matured and began to accumulate "family" into my circle, I never looked upon them as "friends." They were family, and I gave them all the same treatments as I would my biological family. Looking back, I can now say with full conviction that adopting the ones I met along the way into my family was not a wrong decision because I still believe in the concepts I was raised on. However, one must choose carefully because we all come from diverse backgrounds with cultural differences, biases, and experiences.

I have discovered through many tears and gut-wrenching humiliation that each of my friends left me something good to cherish. I will not forget the friends who held my hand when the pain of losing my mother seemed unbearable. I will not forget the ones who brought lunch or dinner or accompanied me somewhere

I felt uncomfortable going alone. I will not forget the ones who called late at night to check up on me and came to visit just to be with me. All of those friends meant something and left me a tiny piece of themselves.

My gift to you: I have come to realize and accept that I cannot control how someone I believed in will behave towards me for the reason they choose to justify. I can dwell on their deceptions and hold those thoughts hostage until they turn me into a bitter old woman…that is my choice.

I have chosen to believe that I have no friend like Jesus. I have chosen to use the experience of those people who deserted me or wronged me in some way as a lesson well-learned because of where I am today. Those people were a part of this journey, and I choose to use their place on the stage of my life as students use their classes. When it is over, we learn, and now we move on.

Do not let negative experiences destroy you. Yes, you crumbled, but now use your hands to set upright the fallen stones of your life. Staying where you fell is not a depiction of the people who tripped you, it is a testament of your own character. Get up and get going and strive to live your best life.

That, my friend, is your gift for today.

I Wonder

Were you shocked
When you heard the news?
What thoughts ran through your mind
When you were told
That I had returned?
Did you wonder
What I would look like?
Did you even think
The old me would resurface?
What did you envisage?
Did you remember
The way we used to be
When there was only you,
The love we shared?
What did you feel?
How did you feel
When our hands clasped?
Did you feel the old electricity
That used to transmit between us?
Did it pass through your fingers?
Does it even matter?
Why should I care
If you felt connected,
If you remembered
How good and solid it used to be?

I wonder what is in your heart,
If it still beats…for me,
If your skin yearns for my touch,
If your lips crave mine.
I will always wonder.

Unwrapping the Gift

Strength for Today

*The Lord is near to the brokenhearted and saves
the crushed in spirit.*

~ Psalm 34:18

Have you ever had a breakup and years later, you see
your old love? Have you ever been let go or fired from a
job and sometime later you see your old boss? Have you
ever left a situation and you see people from your old life?
How did you feel? Especially if you are in a much better
situation than you were and if you have a better job; if you
look more attractive; if the changes in your life are better
than your former life? Did you feel powerful, empowered,
strong, avenged, and absolved?

Sometimes, it is the opposite of the above. You are
not better than your previous situation. You look at your
former love with deep regret because it is your fault the
relationship did not work out and now they are settled

and you want to have the person in your life. You said something, you did something, you let yourself go and you are overweight, not in good health, and the regrets of your past life overshadow you like an unkempt oak tree.

Regrets should be used to motivate and inspire, not used to tear down and beat oneself to death. Use your past regrets and mistakes as stepping stones to make way for a better future. Stare your old self in the face, and confront that image with what you want to be. Move forward with the determination to work towards shedding yourself of the negative habits that caused and resulted in pain and anguish.

My gift to you: You can recover from brokenness. You have to want to be better than you were yesterday. Confront the past with boldness and determination to be better than you previously were. Everyone has a past, and many are not proud of where they have been, but guess what: Your past cannot cling to you if you are determined to let it go. The best way to heal from regret is to learn from it and move on with your life. Getting stuck in the revolving cycle of a hamster's wheel of rethinking and recycling thoughts of the regrets will never allow you to move on. Continue living, and use your regrets as platforms to propel yourself into a better future of lessons well learned.

That, my friend, is your gift for today.

Part 3
The Gift of Healing
And
Letting Go of the Past

Photo credit: D.E.E.

People who hold on to yesterday's hurts like a security blanket do not live, they merely exist.

Heartless

You saw me and felt the connection.
Cautious,
I'm not sure.
The mixed signals
Kept flashing.
I wanted you.
I needed you.
The signs were there.
I refused to look.
You crept closer,
All defenses gone.
You reached over;
You dug into the cavity of my chest
Carefully, calculatingly, searching.
You grabbed and took hold.
You seized and squeezed my heart.
It swelled in your calloused grasp.
Gasping for much-needed air
I cried out…begging you to let go.
You squeezed even harder.
My heart pleaded,
Blood flowing from its eyes.
You kept up the steady torture.
It bled all over the floor.
I had nothing else to give.

You shook it
Till you were satisfied
You got all you needed.
Finally, you slowly let go.
Chills filled my soul,
A relief beyond any other.
Finally,
Glorious warmth
Flooded from my eyes.
You finally let go.

Unwrapping the Gift

Strength for Today

And whenever you stand praying, forgive, if you have anything against anyone, so that your Father also who is in heaven may forgive you your trespasses.

~ Mark 11:25

Has someone ever taken everything you thought you had? In this world, we will meet many takers. They take till they even put some water in your jelly jar and shake it up to get the last bit they can get. Take heart; you still have more to give. Even when people think they have taken the best of you, the best has not been tapped into yet. Sometimes even you, the giver, has not discovered your own goldmine.

Some people come into our lives with one sole purpose: to destroy us. They begin in a subtle way: bringing flowers, showering us with flattering compliments, getting friendly with our children, and before we know it, they have taken control of our lives.

How can I untangle myself from the web I have allowed to be spun around me? You need strength to be able to walk away or to speak up and say, enough. I want better for myself. It takes guts, and yes, you will need to pray as if it is your last prayer. You will get callouses on your knees because you pray so hard and long for deliverance. You may need to cry buckets of tears but rest assured, you can break free. All it is is dominance behavior. You have a bully in your life.

My gift to you: There is no stronghold that cannot be broken. There is no tangled web that cannot be untangled. The big question is: Do you want to be free of the mess you have allowed to be in your life? Are you willing to do what it takes to free yourself and your mind? Pray! Cry! Pray! Cry! Pray, pray, and then speak up! Ask someone you trust to intervene or just be there as you break free. You are a "free born," so don't allow anyone to enslave you. Speak freedom into your soul. Affirm yourself so you can break the chains and walk into a new day where your regrets ignite your soul and usher you into freedom in mind, body, and spirit.

That, my friend, is your gift for today.

Deception

Was it a lie?
When you told me
That you loved me,
That you would always
Be around for me?
Where did those words come from?
Was it a hoax?
Were you just trying to mock me,
Make a mockery of a decades-old friendship?
Who are you,
The person who uttered those acidic words?
Am I dreaming
To think that I gave all I possibly had,
Sharing my family
My time, and my precious heart?
Was it given to a worthless cause?
Should I now be filled
With a fiery anger?
Should I be thankful
That now I know the truth
Sooner than later?
Should I breathe a breath of relief
Knowing your love was never true?
It was a lie.
It was a hoax.

I am not dreaming.
I am burning with a righteous anger
But I am thankful
I get to keep a part of my heart,
The part you threw back at me,
A minute piece of my heart
To help me salvage what is left.
For that, I thank you.

Unwrapping the Gift

Strength for Today

*No one who practices deceit shall dwell in my
house; no one who utters lies shall continue
before my eyes.*

~ Psalm 101:7

Someone lied about me. Someone I trusted.

When someone lies about you and you find out, some-
thing about them dies within you. An established trust
has been broken. We have one thing to give, which is a
fundamental part of who we are. There is no price tag
attached to it: our word. Do what you say you will do. That
sounds so simple, but it is not as simple as it sounds. I hate
being lied to!

People tell you that they love you, but they don't. They love how you make them feel or they love what you can give. They should look out for your best interests, and they should not take advantage of you. We share our hearts and allow people to become a major part of our lives and they prey on us and use the opportunity we have given them to share in the most important aspect of our lives: our families.

When someone deceives you, do not lose heart. They have revealed who they truly are, and that should be a comfort, because the deception is now over. The most difficult part, however, is trying to restore your reputation. This could also be an eye-opener to how people feel about you and how well they really know you. This time of hurt and disappointment must be used to slowly and methodically shrink your circle. Not everyone deserves to be a part of it, and now you have the golden opportunity to clean house.

I have felt the sting of betrayal once too many times and it is almost like a death. Cry and weep for the loss of the friendship, honesty, and the façade they put up which has now crumbled. Take a look at yourself and reevaluate your own priorities and what you desire in a friendship, and do not lower those standards. Pray that you do not allow the deceit to become bitterness and taint the relationships you share with others.

Please do not slander this person's reputation. You must take the high road. A lot of times when situations like this happen, we feel the need to retaliate by sharing intimate details we know of the person. You might actually be an example to them because of how you react.

Sometimes such relationships can be rebuilt, and if that is your case, move forward with the greatest caution. Otherwise, use the experience and only allow people in your circle of friendship who will treasure that gift.

My gift to you: When you are deceived, thank God that you have discovered the truth. We Sierra Leoneans have a saying, "Ninety-nine days for the thief and one day for the man of the house." Translation: Be sure your sins will find you out. Turn every heartache into a lesson well learned.

That, my friend, is your gift for today.

Unresolved

Unexplained feelings,
Thoughts that circulate through my mind
Exploding as they soar.
Unresolved issues,
Hard to solve,
Conflicts converging in unity.
Unexplained
Unresolved
Circulating in my mind.

Unwrapping the Gift

Strength for Today

But the fruit of the Spirit is love, joy, peace, patience, kindness, goodness, faithfulness, gentleness, self-control; against such things there is no law. And those who belong to Christ Jesus have crucified the flesh with its passions and desires. If we live by the Spirit, let us also walk by the Spirit. Let us not become conceited, provoking one another, envying one another.

~ Galatians 5:22–26

Don't you just hate it when you cannot resolve a situation? Soon you are mulling over what happened over and over in your mind, wishing you could have done this or that. Most people find it hard to move on when they have not been allowed to put closure on a situation. Why do you need permission or confrontation for closure? Some situations do not have a resolution. It took me a long time to come to that conclusion. I am a problem-solver so when situations arise, I want them settled so I can solve it and feel accomplished.

There will be times when you just have to let go… walk away from an unresolved issue. Like me, you will feel defeated because you could not satisfy self. I tell you, it will get better. The issue may circulate in your mind for some time and cause you to lose valuable sleep. Walking away is closure. Forgiving yourself is closure. Forgiving the other person is closure. Calling them to yell at them is closure. Writing a letter to express yourself is closure. Whatever you decide to do, let it be the closure that will help to set you free from what happened.

If you do all that is suggested and you still carry the pain of the past, then you can be compared to the man whose jailer opened his cell and told him to leave and be free, but the prisoner refused to leave the prison.

Remember, we will never be in total control when someone else is involved. Letting go strengthens your resolve. Only then will you find peace. Peace comes when I can say I cannot resolve this but I am all right with it. Nothing in your past is worth agonizing over. It is PAST. It happened yesterday. Let it go so you can live. People who hold on to yesterday's hurts do not live, they merely exist. Pray and ask God to help you let it go. Ask God for strength to see you through, and put a period behind it and use that as closure.

My gift to you: When a situation occurs and relationships end, take it as prison doors flung wide and your jailor asking you to leave the premises. Do not ask them why it is time to walk out into the sunshine and make other choices. Always remember that moving forward is closure, and you do not need to confront a person to get closure; closure is an action and state of mind, so move forward and live.

That, my friend, is your gift for today.

Worthy of Love

Sadness:
Feeling empty inside,
Empty as a house
Without furniture,
No love or care.
Messed up:
Torn from the inside out.
Sadness:
To be alive yet dead,
Decaying inside,
Yet you stole.
Yes, you stole my joy.
Only for a moment:
A long, slow, painful moment
Of defeat.
Yet, I arise,
My freedom banner I raise up high,
I proclaim it.
I am free!
Free to love.
Free to give love and receive.
Free to be filled again.
Free to turn these horrible moments,
To free past memories.
I am worthy of this moment.

I have reclaimed my joy,
My worth.
I am free.
Free.

Unwrapping the Gift

Strength for Today

Brothers, if anyone is caught in any transgression, you who are spiritual should restore him in a spirit of gentleness. Keep watch on yourself, lest you too be tempted. Bear one another's burdens, and so fulfill the law of Christ. For if anyone thinks he is something, when he is nothing, he deceives himself.

~ Galatians 6:1–3

Have you ever felt you are not worth it? You are not worthy of your job, your family, love, and even God's amazing grace? We sometimes feel that we are not good enough to get what we have. Why is it that I am being promoted? Why was I offered the position? Why does he love me? What does she want with me? We sometimes feel that we are so stained that our sin cannot be blotted out. Why?

Where does this deep-rooted feeling of lack come from? Was it when we were overlooked at the playground? Was it when our parents gave something we wanted to our siblings and we felt less than?

A friend once told me of the repeated abuse she received from a series of men over a long period of time. It was back in the day when to speak out about rape was a stigma to the victim, as well as to their family. Whenever a girl was brave enough to speak out, the family disregarded the claim and brushed it under the rug.

My friend decayed inside while the rest of her family went about their daily lives as if nothing had happened and continued to happen. She also spiraled into sleeping around with countless others, trying to numb her crushed and broken spirit through sex.

After years of counselling, my friend has found solace and joy in Christ. When the past is held tightly in our hands, we cannot let go to make room for something else, something new. I do not think anyone who has ever been abused will ever forget what happened to them. I do believe that it is possible to rise above and move beyond what happened, with the right help and the willingness to let go. It may take years to reclaim your freedom physically and mentally. If you are willing, you can reclaim your life. Soon, you can love and have joy, which will transform your life.

My gift to you: No one on this planet is better than you unless you want them to be. Take a good look in the mirror; that person you see there is you. Yes, you! You are amazing. You are wonderful! You.

That, my friend, is your gift for today.

My Shame

You took
What was mine
To give.
You ripped it out of my grasp.
That makes you
A thief.
You took my greatest gift.
What else do I have to render?
I have wallowed too long
In this mire
Of self-pity,
The bog of deception.
I've allowed myself
To fall victim
To this quicksand of depression.
This quagmire
You dug for me,
Your creation.
Now I refuse
To give you any more.
I still have life.
I will
Find peace.
I will find joy.
One day,

I will find love.
One day,
I will be whole again.
My house will be filled; this body of mine
Will be filled
With laughter,
With joy.
As soon as my mind sets me free.

Unwrapping the Gift

Strength for Today

The Lord is near to the brokenhearted and saves the crushed in spirit.

~ Psalm 34:18

We cannot pray all of our troubles away. The mind is a powerful tool, and sometimes we are trapped in the prisons of the mind. Many times, we do not have any control over the horrible incidents that happen to us in this life. We have control over how we deal with it and how we are able to move forward in our lives so that we can have meaningful relationships that are free of the holds and entanglements of yesterday's curses.

I am well aware that some things are easier to pray over, along with counseling, than others, including recovering from a rape, abuse in all forms, discrimination, etc. I recall a friend telling me that every time she saw any man she thought of the man who had raped her over fifteen years before. It did not matter if the man was her pastor or a priest. I cried with my friend as she recounted the incident and as she claimed the blame for a sick, twisted individual's brutal actions against her that fateful evening. I encouraged her to seek professional help and eventually, she did, but she continues to struggle and suffer with the shame. I am sure some of us have our own struggles we think we can never overcome. There is no sorrow we can face that heaven cannot heal.

I could not even begin to fathom my friend's anguish each time she saw a man, and she had to relive the experience. My only source of comfort to her was to hold her close and tell her of God's love: a love so pure and true that his Son, Jesus, came to earth and died for all of us. This is a love that is unquestioned. I cannot put to words the anguish men and women go through because of the unthinkable actions of others, and I want you to know that this section is the hardest to write because I have heard of the deep turmoil of so many people in this world. My only consolation is to share God's love for you and for me.

I have had many hurts, and my only source of consolation through my despair has been the deep faith and assurance I have in the God I serve.

My gift to you: Living in the suffocating stranglehold of yesterday is a self-created prison we can break free from. The pain of the past is real, and taking baby steps backwards and away from the pain will bring healing and peace. Someone's evil action towards you is not your fault.

You can be restored and made whole when you are willing to try. There is no easy road to recovery, but chaining yourself to a painful situation is giving the wrongdoer power, and you need to reclaim that power. There is healing in the power of God and the deliverance of full assurance that there is no sorrow that heaven cannot heal. Take hold of that assurance as you strive to find peace.

That, my friend, is your gift for today.

Betrayal

You have taken my breath away.
For once, I do not know what to say.
My heart flutters as I replay
All the scenes that went awry.
I am wounded deeply
Since you have taken
My love so cheaply.
What a shame
It was not treasured,
Even by me,
Even though
It was given in full measure.
How will this broken heart mend?
What a crime; I must now deal,
Even with this broken zeal,
This betrayal
Has brought me
Down on my knees.
Recovering from betrayal
Is devastating,
Like a death,
Stealing a person's breath,
Tragic like Macbeth.
For once, I do not know what to say
Since you have now taken

My love so cheaply.
What a crime to deal with,
Like a death.
No turning back
To what once was.
Trust gone.
Trust gone.
Trust all gone.

Unwrapping the Gift

Strength for Today

In return for my love they accuse me, but I give myself to prayer.

~ Psalm 109:4

Betrayal feels like a stab in the back by someone we trusted and gave full access into our lives. Betrayal hurts on many levels because a lot of times, the person who betrays us was trusted to uphold our innermost thoughts and deepest secrets. This is someone you would have gone to the guillotine to proclaim their innocence for, and now they have divulged something about you that no one else knew. They have not stood up for you. They have joined others to castigate you. They have maligned you. They have lied to others about you. You thought they would be there for you, and now their true colors have surfaced and it hurts in a way you cannot even express.

My gift to you: When someone betrays our trust, they have shown who they are. We feel it in our depths because we feel stupid for trusting that individual. When we are betrayed, the last thing on our minds is a dance of thanksgiving that this person has revealed their true selves. However, thank God that they showed who they were because look at the brighter side; you could have told them or opened your heart wider than you did. Take heart, and thank God you now know who and what the person truly is. Betrayal is not a lack of your character, it is the revelation of the betrayer's character.

That, my friend, is your gift for today.

My Regret

A cold feeling of guilt
Washed over me
As I looked in her section
Of the room.
Over there it was cold,
Dark and dreary,
Complicated by lies
That had been told.
It seemed like just yesterday
We would dare each other
To roam around tombstones
Seeking ghosts and goblins.
Her confession
Brought back the pain and misery
Of forgotten dreams;
Of broken hope and promises
That we thought had all faded away.
Distracted by the dampness in the air,
I struggle to imagine
How it used to be
Before deceit
Wrecked our idealistic existence;
A license
To abandon what could have been.
My gaze returns

To the pathetic figure
Huddled in the space of time and mind.
I weep bitterly
For the child locked up inside.
I mourn the loss of this aborted dream.

Unwrapping the Gift

Strength for Today

Their throat is an open grave; they use their tongues to deceive. The venom of asps is under their lips.

~ Romans 3:13

Some time ago, as I sat in a restaurant enjoying time alone, I saw someone walk by that I had a close relationship with in the past. She did not see me, and I watched her as she browsed the items that were at the entrance of the opposite store, and my mind took flight to the past. I remembered us building our relationship and making plans for our future. We had planned to take vacations with our families and shared advice on raising our children.

As I watched her, I saw how she had aged, and I wondered if she saw me, what she would think about. Would she think whether the years had been kind to me? I still saw the things I liked about her from our past, and I also conjured to my mind why we were no longer friends. I thought about going out and signaling to her and asking her to join me. Then I remembered the pain, the hurt, the feelings of betrayal, and I quickly thrust that thought from my mind and just continued to watch her till she moved on and out of my sight.

My gift to you: There are some people we thought would always be a part of our lives and today they are no longer a part of our lives, or we are not as close as we used to be. It has become cliché that people come into our lives for a reason, and also a season, and when that is accomplished, they move on. Whatever you have heard, when friendships are not maintained, we hurt for their loss. The value of the relationship remains the same. Gold does not lose its value because the luster is dim from use. What you have shared remains valuable in the lessons of your life. Those lessons will propel you to a better future.

That, my friend, is your gift for today.

Purification

Regret knocked at her door,
Waiting for a chance
To sit back down and wallow.
Her muddled thoughts
Scrambled for cover
As they receded
Into the caverns of the past.
Then anger raised her ugly head,
Looking over the events
That brought us here.
Emotions could no longer
Keep tears at bay.
They began to fall
Unheedingly,
Unstoppable,
Flowing down her cheeks.
The rivets of the dam
Came undone,
No longer bound
By that strong front
Presented to the world.
The ugliest of twisted mouth,
The so-called Ugly Cry,
The unsightliness of tears and snot
Converging to emerge

Together in the crevice of her neck.
Unhinged and dismantled,
No longer held back by propriety,
The wrenching ache of ribs and gut
Cleansing out the hurt,
Disappointment and pain,
Sobbing anguish,
Slowly,
Quietly,
Calmly.
It is over.
The storm has passed.
A new soul emerges
Stronger,
Resilient,
Cleansed and free.

Unwrapping the Gift

Strength for Today

Fear not, for I am with you; be not dismayed, for I am your God; I will strengthen you, I will help you, I will uphold you with my righteous right hand.

~ Isaiah 41:10

I was angry. If I was the person I used to be twenty-five years ago, I would have considered physically hurting that person so they could also feel the pain and hurt I was going through right then.

I hated the fact that I was devastated over the words I was reading on my computer screen. Very hurtful words had been written, and I kept replaying them over and over in my mind until I could read that letter verbatim to you.

I always prided myself in being the best friend a person would ever have, and someone I love took a sledgehammer and crushed me and my award. The words I read that day crushed me like a sack of stones called a reality check.

My gift to you: It took me a while to regroup, and then I realized that I had taken credit for my ability to be friends with people that others found abrasive and unlovable. I had a puffed-out chest at my ability, and I forgot some important lessons. I did not thank God for the ability he had given me, and I had failed to follow the rules. Sometimes people come into our lives and we are to interact with them, but only for a season. We all know that, but for some strange reason I, who thought I had it all figured out, had forgotten. Do not let your pride get in the way of common sense.

That, my friend, is your gift for today.

The Owl

There he goes again,
Shouting at the top
Of his lungs.
There he pounds and beats on his chest
As he surveys
His domain.
There he goes again,
Remembering yesterday's loss;
The mouse that got away.
There he sits…
Pondering,
Listening to night sounds,
Swiftly moving…slowly, silently.
There he goes again,
Swooping and catching his prey.
There he goes again.
Triumphant.

Unwrapping the Gift

Strength for Today

Bless the Lord, O my soul, and forget not all his benefits, who forgives all your iniquity, who heals all your diseases, who redeems your life from the pit, who crowns you with steadfast love and mercy.

~ Psalm 103:2–4

Every time I glance back into the negativity, sadness, and destruction of my past life, I have allowed the enemy to triumph. If you have lived for a considerable amount of time, you have probably racked up some deeds that you are not proud of. We have an adversary who will bring those things we want to forget into memory every time we are feeling successful and we think we are better than we were in our past. Memories of the things we want to remain hidden in the annals of our memory banks will resurface at the least opportune times and jerk us back in painful displays of regret.

It seems like each time I move forward in victory and relief in my newfound joy and freedom with the Lord, a memory will come across my mind and throw me back into the grasp of yesterday and its regrets. Often I feel the clutches of the past clawing at me and dragging its claws down my back.

My gift to you: I am always amazed at how the enemy will bring thoughts of my past to remembrance in moments when I feel that I am doing very well in my life. When I am confident in who I am and proud of my accomplishments is when the enemy will try to throw sand in my Farina. We must stare the past in the eye and say to it, "News flash: Jesus died for that sin too!" You cannot keep holding a debt over my head that has already been repaid.

That, my friend, is your gift for today.

Life after Death: My Son

Nothing prepares us to face death.
The finality of death
Leaves an ache
No one can calm,
No word can soothe.
Nothing prepares us to face death,
Stare it in the face,
Stand up tall
Stick out one's chest,
Stick up one's fist.
We had hopes
That one day
You would become a man,
That God could say,
That is a man after my own heart.
Nothing prepares us to face death,
The cold,
The stillness,
The lifelessness,
The finality.
Nothing prepares us to face death.
The ache is constant.
Unending, wrenching pain
Is what I feel
Each day I awaken without you.

My son,
We prayed
That your oath would
Remain straight
That we can rejoice,
Because God can get all the glory and praise.
Nothing prepares us to face death,
No matter how many others we have faced
Or the distance between.
Time does not ease the hurt.
Time is not a balm for the heart.
My son,
We had hopes and we prayed.
God answered each of our prayers.
God took you when all was right with you.
Nothing prepares us to face death.
We face it and cling
To each other and to
God.
Nothing prepares us to face death.

Unwrapping the Gift

Strength for Today

This is my comfort in my affliction, that your promise gives me life.

-Psalm 119: 50

Blessed be the God and Father of our Lord Jesus Christ, the Father of mercies and God of all comfort.

~ 2 Corinthians 1:3

Ryan has passed!

Those words were a cut so deep I now wonder how I made it through those three words. As I write this section I am so filled with hurt, and I've cried some too.

I had thought, if I get there, I would say, "Hey, baby, Mom is here. Wake up!" and everything would be all right. I was Superhero Mom, and I was going to save the day. God had other plans.

I was not going to make it to Sierra Leone where my son was in a coma from cerebral malaria. I would not see my vibrant son alive; all I would have now are the memories of him to comfort me.

I was devastated. My heart was shattered in uncountable pieces, and even those pieces were shattered too.

Some of my closest friends said they didnt call because they didn't want to overwhelm me since they knew everyone else was calling.

I am learning a lot about myself during my time of grief. The people who I thought knew me did not know me at all. For those of you who understand my psyche, you know that I am looking within to analyze my part in this misunderstanding. Have I misrepresented myself if my own friends do not know that I needed them to just be there?

Losing Ryan has been my deepest and all-consuming loss, and it is also the incident that has brought me closer to God. Each day after the tremendous loss, I would be floating between sanity and insanity. I could not understand, and on many mornings, I would awake with tears on my face. I have wept so many tears for the loss of my son, and then the tears dried up on the outside and stayed inside till I felt like I was drowning. I am so grateful that I am a Christian. I have clung to Scripture because no one's words could bring me comfort. God's Word through his promises has kept me going.

I am alone. I realize I am alone in my grief because no two people can feel the same way about losing the same loved one. You can empathize, but you will never know what I am going through. I am hurting, and this is when the only source of strength is the word of God found in the Scriptures of the Bible. The disappointment in people is just a reaction, sometimes a misplaced reaction, from the deep hurt of the loss.

When someone loses someone to death, remember that there are no words you can utter to make them feel better. If they are in front of you, just hold them close and hug them. You can call them and just say I am so sorry for your loss. Send them a card and put some money in it, because the person will have expenses and they will need assistance with. Please do not ask them what happened, tell them you know how they feel, or start talking about a loss you have also suffered. Whatever else you do, please do not quote Scripture to the person. If the person chooses to cry, let them get it out and do not tell them it will get better. When people lose their loved ones to death, remember, they will hurt for a long time, so check on them often.

Death is not like a bad toothache which the dentist can fill or extract and you are relieved. Death is your own heart being ripped out of your chest and you start to bleed from the cut but the bleeding does not stop. If you are not careful to cut off the bleeding heart, you might bleed to death.

My gift to you: Losing a child is one of the worst pains a person can ever endure, so if you are a friend to a grieving parent, check often, and let your friend know that you care. I will always cry thinking of Ryan but trusting that God blessed us with him and we should be grateful we had a child calling us Mom and Dad is my everlasting gratitude. Each time I think of my son, I say "Thank you, Father, for giving us our gift." We must always be grateful that the ones who have left us were in our lives in the first place. Being grateful puts everything in a different perspective.

That, my friend, is your gift for today.

Part 4
The Gift of Blessings

Photo credit: Ryan Ellis

If you live with eternity in the forefront of your mind, you will be kinder, gentler, and live with purpose in your stride. So... live well!

It's Monday

The sun woke me up this morning
With a smile.
The morning sky winked at me
As I stepped out the door.
The lined road full of palm trees
Told me to hurry on to work.
The traffic lights flashing
Green, red, and orange
Told me to watch out and watch my speed.
I arrived at my destination.
She welcomed me back to Monday morning.
I love Monday mornings.

~ * ~

Unwrapping the Gift

Strength for Today

The Lord make his face to shine upon you and be gracious to you; the Lord lift up his countenance upon you and give you peace. "So shall they put my name upon the people of Israel, and I will bless them."

~ Numbers 6:25–27

I love Mondays! My friends and family always ask me the big question: WHY?

Why would anyone love the day most of us have to return to our jobs after a weekend? I love Mondays because I am at my very best on Mondays. I have been given an opportunity to step back from my regular work week with a weekend. I have focused on my family and myself and most importantly, I have been to church to share in fellowship with other Christians and have been inspired to be my best self through the sermon that was preached. I have had the bread of life, and now I am equipped and ready to face the week head-on. I am my very best on Mondays.

What is your superpower? We are asked this as educators. Mine is the word of God. I am unapologetically a Christian. I will not be as bold as to say I am always at my best, but I strive each day to uphold Christian standards, and what better day than Monday to get the ball rolling? Mondays, after the recharging of my spirit, I am geared up and ready for the challenges of the week. How about you? What particular day of the week do you love? Each day is a new day to live the life we have been created to live. We should always strive to be our very best selves.

It is also a mindset. Sometimes, we tend to follow others who say they hate certain days of the week. Ask yourself, why do you like certain days and hate others? Have a reason for yourself and then, think of all the blessings you have; to be given the opportunity to go to work and have the ability to care for yourself and your family. Think of countless others who would gladly trade places with you. Yes, I know some people are difficult to work with. How about you? Are you a difficult person to work with? Do you make the workspace easier for others to collaborate and accomplish the goals of the organization you work for?

My gift to you: Be grateful for the day. It's a gift in itself. You are here, and you are valued. Each day should be a day of thanksgiving, not just to be alive, not just on Monday, but every day. I strive to live each day with eternity in mind. I ask myself each day, "If this is my last day, at the end of the day, would I say I lived my best today?" If you live with glory after death in the forefront of your mind, you will be kinder, gentler, accommodating, and living with purpose and gratitude. Live well!

That, my friend, is your gift for today.

Prepared

Is anyone ever prepared
For the great transition,
Moving from being a child,
Striding into adolescence?
Is anyone ever prepared?
Change from elementary,
Propelled into equidistant
With its set of rules
For the greater good of all.
Is anyone ever prepared
To face the diversity,
The change and culture shock,
The read aloud
And think aloud?
Is anyone ever really prepared?
Facing the uncertainty
Of pronunciations,
The horror stories
Of bullies and detestable school lunches.
Is anyone ever really prepared?
No one is ever really prepared
To challenge the monster school,
The mountainous books,
The change of classes,
The exposure to varying exceptionalities.

No one is ever really prepared.
Most are willing
And able to face the challenges,
Able to stick their chest out,
Not really prepared for this new world;
Not really prepared,
But willing to try.

Unwrapping the Gift

Strength for Today

Let those who delight in my righteousness shout for joy and be glad and say evermore, "Great is the Lord, who delights in the welfare of his servant!"

~ Psalm 35:27

I am not sure about you, but I was so ready to grow up –but I was not prepared to grow up. There was a time I wanted to get away from home and start the business of being grown. It took a little while to realize that growing up meant I had to use the skills my parents and family members taught me to stay in the life-changing process. I made some horrible decisions as I tried to be grown and not ask for advice and assistance when I needed it most. I did not know that being grown also meant being smart enough to run home and talk to my parents or my siblings to ask for guidance.

We have all been there, where we think we are ready to leave home, move into our own spaces and begin acting like we have good sense when we actually do not. For many, shame and pride cause them not to call on their family or an adult who has already traveled the grown-up route to help them.

My gift to you: As you move from one stage of life to the next, you will need assistance at every level. No matter how mature you are, you will need someone to celebrate with you, stand with you when others are against you, and most importantly, have someone who can give godly advice that will give you hope and courage to keep moving forward. Realizing that no one makes it through life without the help of others should help tear the walls of pride down so you can humble yourself and ask for help. You will go further when you acknowledge that there are good people in your life who can help you make it to your promised land.

That, my friend, is your gift for today.

Stars

Some people
Like to look at the stars;
Takes them
Long to find the constellations.
Artists draw
Stars depicted in their paintings.
Researchers
Rediscover as they seek truth.
Stars shine bright,
Leaving with guiding
On a dark path.

Unwrapping the Gift

Strength for Today

Every good gift and every perfect gift is from above, coming down from the Father of lights with whom there is no variation or shadow due to change.

~ James 1:17

As a young girl, I used to read my horoscope and pattern my life according to it. When a boy showed an interested in me, I wanted to know what his Zodiac sign was to know if we were "aligned" to avoid wasting my time. Now I look back and just laugh at my naivety. I would read that I should "shield my field and that the skies feature a harmonious hook up of the sensitive moon and reactive Venus." What does that even mean?

I am cautioned to "be extra susceptible to people's moods and opinions, and it will be hard to stay centered." I read that I should "do my best to either hunker down in my own safe haven, whether that is my home or someone else's. Even on calls, cut the toxic types a wide berth. They have a way to push your buttons regardless of what you do."

Reading that horoscope, I would excuse the bad behaviors of those around me because the horoscope already forewarned me. I would cut people out that I thought were toxic and make way for those who would push my buttons. Looking back, I had a very shallow existence based on what someone says the stars told them about how I should live my life.

Now you know why I laugh about my past relationship with horoscopes. It was not hard to leave the world of mystic stargazing behind me after some of the readings were just too bizarre and could not possibly be for me. Because of a profoundly deeper understanding of the One who told me that he has ordered my steps, my life and the world are in his hands, and I live in complete hope and trust in God. The freedom of being a Christian is not having to worry about anything that is going on or that will happen in my life because my Heavenly Father has me completely covered.

My gift to you: The God who created the stars has you and your life in the palm of his hands. If God created the world and all of us, how would he give another thing to shine to provide light for us and replace him in being our ultimate guide? The stars are meant to provide light so we can see our way. The stars were never meant to guide our lives and the way we live; they shine so we can see. God is the one who made the stars tells them when to shine. Trust the God who made the stars.

That, my friend, is your gift for today.

The Freedom Train

Wading through the muck
Of oppression that lingers.
My spirit clashes
With that of thoughtless men
Who oppose Freedom's train,
That ejaculated emancipation,
Their callousness reflected
In the grandeur
Of their created status quo,
Palatial
Plantations
Filled and overflowing with blood.
These relatives
Of bloodthirsty gladiators.
Their only thought
Is geared towards demoralizing
Those who are helpers and debased
By cruelty and inhumane acts
To those who dare to disobey.
Taking a stand
Against injustice,
Lending voice to countless others,
Praying that one day
The muck will clear up and
Freedom train's wheels

Will once more turn,
Taking all men:
Free and enslaved,
To the judgment hall.

Unwrapping the Gift

Strength for Today

Give, and it will be given to you. Good measure, pressed down, shaken together, running over, will be put into your lap. For with the measure you use it will be measured back to you.

~ Luke 6:38

When I analyze the degree of unspoken social oppression that exists in our world, I am sickened. We talk to our children about not being bullies and speaking up for the downtrodden. How many of us will speak out when we see other humans being maltreated by our police, teachers, other students, and even the president? The question here, however, is what is holding you back from standing up for someone who possibly cannot stand up for themselves?

I am a proud American, and I will not allow that citizenship of gratitude to cloud my sense of duty to humankind. Our society has a need to overpower and gain status and wealth over others around us. All of that is good—if you are going about it the correct way. We can all work hard to accomplish our dreams but it should not be at the detriment of those who are less fortunate than we are.

My gift to you: We will definitely reap what we sow. Sometimes we think we are on top, and we can never be down again because we have surpassed the lower rungs of the ladder. Let us not forget that God lifts and he also lowers. There is not a single person living under God's sun who will not reap what they sow. When you stand on the sidelines seeing injustice and turning a blind eye, you are also supporting and promoting the injustice. If you have blood running through your veins, you are human. If, when you are cut with a sharp object, blood oozes out, then you are human. If you can feel hurt, then never forget that others, regardless of race or creed, also feel similar emotions and hurt. This realization should call out to your humanity, and if it does not, start looking deep down and asking yourself why it does not.

That, my friend, is your gift for today.

My Peace for You: My Child

Fear not, my child,
I am here for you.
No need to be scared,
I am right here beside you
Where I have always been.
Take care not, my child,
My promises are for sure.
When I told you
That I will never leave you
Nor forsake you,
I meant every word.
Hold on tightly
To my promises;
My word,
It never breaks.
Be strong now, my child.
The long days are going to be
Long
And
Hard.
There will be pain.
There will be tears.
There will be fear.
But remember,
I am always with you.

Trust in me
To see you through
It all.
Have peace now, my child,
The peace
Only I alone can give.
Rest in the knowledge
Of my unfailing love
That I will carry you
Over the rough patches.
Fear not.
Take care.
Be strong.
I am with you.
Have peace now, my child.

Unwrapping the Gift

Strength for Today

Beloved, I pray that all may go well with you and that you may be in good health, as it goes well with your soul.

~ 3 John 1:2

For eighteen months, I was burdened by my medical condition. At first when the issue began, I diagnosed it as the stress I was undergoing at my job. Then a few relationships I had cultivated over my lifetime unraveled, and I thought that was the cause for my body going through the devastation, hurt, instability, and mental trauma.

Then, when the months ensued and the issue persisted, I sought the consult of my doctors and that began a long road of second, third, and fourth opinions and the arduous road of rethinking and discovery. As I moved from one doctor to the next, I began to lose heart. I did not say faith, I said I began to lose heart. I became discouraged.

I am very good at masking my pain, and I have perfected the art of only letting people see what I want them to see.

Then one day at Costco, I was looking at the selection of books they carried and saw the *Dear Jesus* book and I started reading it and realized that Jesus had been talking to me all this time, and like an errant child, I had heard him but not listened. I bought the book and read it.

As I read, I could feel God's love for me and got the comfort of knowing that no matter what issue I was going through, God wanted me to trust him. He wanted me to depend on him and to believe that every word he speaks through his Word, the Bible, is the absolute truth. The promises that are in the word of God are true.

I began to find peace, then joy, and finally, total reliance that my Father will see me through what he wants me to endure.

My gift to you: Do you doubt God's love? Do you feel alone and forsaken in your circumstances? No matter what is happening in your life, God's got you! You can rely on family and friends and even doctors, but as a child of God, God's got you.

That, my friend, is your gift for today.

Our Time

It is early morn.
I awaken,
Restless,
Sweaty,
Aches and pains
All over my body.
I call to you.
This is our home.
The time I feel
So close to you;
I feel your presence
As I marvel
At your strength.
This time,
Our time together,
I feel your power
As you whisper
Softly
To calm my fears,
Firmly
To affirm your authority,
Quietly
To still my quivering soul.
You speak,
I've got you.

There is nothing to fear.
Rest now in my care.
Find comfort in my strength.
Find peace in my blessed assurance.
Find rest in my sovereignty.
This is our time.
Rest now, my child.
Rest well.

Unwrapping the Gift

Strength for Today

When a man's ways please the Lord, he makes even his enemies to be at peace with him.

~ Proverbs 16:7

I have always been an early riser, and that time in the morning when all is still and everyone is fast asleep is when I feel closest to God. I feel like it is just him and I alone and intimate, and I can pour myself out to him and stay still so that he can talk to me in the quietness of my mind.

I grew up in a Christian home, and God's presence was introduced to me and I have witnessed as it transforms and restores lives. I have also experienced how, when

I handed over my life to God, he turned it around and gave me peace.

It was morning, like the ones I share now with him, when I did not know where I was going, and even though I had dreams and goals, my mind was in a constant turmoil. One morning, I just broke down and said to him, "God, I am tired of driving this bus of my life. It seems as if I am driving a Mega Bus, and I have only the training to drive a mini-van, and I have lost control of this and I am drowning."

It seemed as if a warm cloth was placed over my feverish brow and cool hands brushed over my shoulder and patted me on the back as I felt engulfed by God's love.

That was the turning point, and even though every now and then I try to take the keys of the Mega Bus out of God's hands, He still continues to soothe me and whispers to me, "'For I know the plans I have for you,' declares the LORD, "'plans to prosper you and not to harm you, plans to give you hope and a future'" (Jer. 29:11).

My gift to you: When you call on God, He will hear you and come to your aid, but you must be still so you can hear him. Your faith and trust is proven when you allow God to come through at his time, for he has plans to prosper you. God has plans to give you hope and a future, and all you have to do is let him lead and guide you.

That, my friend, is your gift for today.

Total Reliance

Such a peace
I have found
To finally realize
There is no need to worry
Nor fret,
Even to be concerned,
Which is the
Worry.
This is not mine
To carry.
Never thought that before!
Total reliance
Means
Total dependency
On you,
Giving up my will,
Submitting,
Giving it all
Totally,
Completely,
To you.
So I can evolve
From uncertainty
To a trusting,
Dependent child

Who relies
Totally,
Completely
On her Father
Who supplies her every need.
Totally reliant on you.

Unwrapping the Gift

Strength for Today

For it is God who works in you, both to will and to work for his good pleasure.

~ Philippians 2:13

There have been times when I struggled with taking control of my own life, even though I knew that I had handed it over to God and had asked him to take the driver's seat of my life. I told God I trusted him to direct my path, but for some reason, every now and then, I want to drive my own life and without fail, things never go the way I planned.

Total reliance on God is like the child who realizes it will not eat if his mother does not feed him. God wants us to place our trust in him. To give him everything so he can steer us where he wants us to be. God wants to guide us through the valleys where we sometimes undergo trials, and he carries us or he takes us to the mountaintop so others can see what he has done for us and they too can come to be under the shadow of his mighty wings.

My gift to you: When we totally place our dependency on the Lord, we do not need to worry about the issues in life because he will never leave us and he will never forsake us. Trust God and hand yourself over to him. It is exhausting running around on your own steam and never getting anywhere. Hand your life to God, and receive a peace you never can imagine exists. You will thank me.

That, my friend, is your gift for today.

The Fight

I came out swinging,
Fighting,
Slugging.
I came out
Like a bull out of the pen.
I came out swinging;
You slung back.
Unsuspecting,
I fell to the ground
Mouthful
Of your fist.
You slung back.
Hard.
Why fight when
I can lay here
In my defeat?
No more blows.
I can rest to fight
Another day.
Tomorrow
I will come out fighting.

Unwrapping the Gift

Strength for Today

Show yourself in all respects to be a model of good works, and in your teaching show integrity, dignity.

~ Titus 2:7

So many times, I have watched students fight each other over a serious issue like bullying, or a not so serious issue like you stole my boyfriend or you gossiped about me, and now I felt disrespected by you. The question is always, "Did you tell an adult about this so that we could intervene and not have the conflict come to this point?"

"I can handle this by myself," they say. Handling it by yourself has resulted in an out of school suspension, medical bills for your parents, a bruised ego because you got beat up, or shame because someone videotaped the incident and posted it on social media.

So many times, issues occur in our lives that can be handled by the grieved voicing their displeasure and having a mediator try to help both parties resolve the issues that have arisen. We want to fight our own battles and gloat in our ill-gained victories. How can we gloat over an ill-gained victory? It is ideal when two people who made a child or children together can co-parent amicably, sharing the responsibilities of their creation. That would be the ideal situation. Then you have the other side of that amicability. When one parent is not as committed as the other and fails to carry their responsibility and conveniently forgets that they have a child or children and that they are responsible for their wellbeing. Your overall goal is to see that your children are wholesome and that they grow to be loving and responsible adults.

My gift to you: We are responsible to take care of the children God has entrusted into our care. When we raise our children to have self-esteem and respect themselves and others, we have won half the battle. Our children are one of our most precious treasures and we must treat them as such.

That, my friend, is my gift to you.

Baby Sister: My Gift

You came into my life
When I was not expecting you.
So bright
You radiated
Warmth,
Vitality,
And a spirit
So full of life.
My sister;
Baby sister.
I knew my purpose,
My goal,
Was to care for you,
Comfort,
Defend,
Love you at all and any cost.
You were sent to me
To give me a different perspective,
A softness of heart.
My sister;
Baby sister.
I see you
And I see myself
Mirrored,
Strong,

Sometimes uncertain,
So talented,
Yet unsure.
Great heart,
My sister;
Baby sister, you were sent to me
For me.
That is okay,
To live a bit for me.
To care for myself,
To live this life
To God's fullest will.
My sister;
Baby sister
To cry if I need to.
To allow myself to be weak
And not be ashamed to show it,
To get help
Even when I do not think I need it,
To allow someone into my heart,
Into my life.
My sister;
Baby sister.
You let me be myself.
You demanded I let my hair down,
Let my defenses down,
To be loved…and love again.
Accepted,
To connect
In a way that is foreign to me.
You were sent to me

By the One who gives perfect gifts,
My sister;
Baby sister.
My own gift.

Unwrapping the Gift

Strength for Today

Not that I am speaking of being in need, for I have learned in whatever situation I am to be content. I know how to be brought low, and I know how to abound. In any and every circumstance, I have learned the secret of facing plenty and hunger, abundance and need.

~ Philippians 4:11–12

Over the years, God has provided me many gifts, and one of the most precious he sent me was a little sister. She is not biologically mine, but it sure feels like it. I met my baby sister when she and I needed a sister's love. Living away from my birth home of Sierra Leone, I often miss my sisters, and as the years have gone by, I am not as close to my younger sisters as I desire. They have their own families and are living their own lives, even though we talk on the phone. I often wonder how different things would be if we were all together in the same country. When I see others with their sisters, I feel a particular loss because even though I know we share the love of siblings, we are not as close because of the distance and the way our lives have evolved.

Biologically, I have eight sisters and they are all so different in personality and temperament, and even though I am closest to one of my older sisters (my kindred spirit), I often regret not being closer to them.

When I met my baby sister, I knew God sent her to me for a specific purpose. She opened my eyes to see things differently, from a younger person's perspective, and my purpose is to care for her emotionally and spiritually.

My gift to you: When God sends you a gift and you see it for what it is, accept it and thank God for what he has provided; you have been blessed. Who is in your life that you are to influence positively? Things do not happen by happenchance for a Christian. God has fashioned our lives, and he puts people and situations in our lives to fulfill a bigger purpose. Everyone you come in contact with is meant to either bless you or for you to fulfill a blessing in their life.

That, my friend, is your gift for today.

2:00 A.M.

Turning over in my bed,
I wake up.
It must be 2:00 a.m.
Slowly, I stretch,
Trying not to catch a cramp.
It must be 2:00 a.m.
Carefully,
I swing my legs down
To the floor.
I reach down to touch my toes.
It must be 2:00 a.m.
I walk the short distance,
Take care of nature's call.
It has to be 2:00 a.m.
Quietly,
I make my way
Back to my base,
Crawl back under the covers.
It is 2:00 a.m.
I am prostrate.
It is 2:00 a.m.
My face down
And thank you
For touching me,
Waking me up.

This is my favorite time
With you.
It is 2:00 a.m.
This is the time I call
Our time;
Our time to talk,
When I pour out my soul,
Telling you what
You already know.
Yes, it is 2:00 a.m.
Asking you to grant me favors;
Favors you have already given answers for.
Yes. No. Not yet.
It is 2:00 a.m.
Seeking your guidance.
You are always willing.
Discernment.
I'm prostrate before you,
Quiet,
Still,
I listen as you speak.
This is our time.
2:00 a.m.
It is 2:00 a.m.
It is just you and I.
It is just you and I.

Unwrapping the Gift

Strength for Today

And endurance produces character, and character produces hope.

~ Romans 5:4

I always get the question, "Why are you up so early?" My body has been trained to get up when it has had enough rest is my usual answer. But I can also add that it is time to be awake and get my day started. I have already shared with you that the wee hours of the morning are when I feel closest to God. I have always treasured my personal prayer time with God when I have the feeling that he is only with me, and I have him all to myself.

Two a.m. seems to be the time for my meetup with God. I am always so very happy when I can just pour myself out and tell him not only my concerns, but one of the most pleasing things to do is to just share with him my victories. Lord, thank you because this week I did not cry as much over my loss. Thank you for holding my hand as I confronted that bully and made my displeasure clear. I am so grateful that you saw me through a difficult meeting, a breakup, a disappointment. Lord, please help me to reflect on your Word and seek your instruction, and I ask you to help me as I grasp your peace and cling to it for sustenance.

I love my private time with God.

My gift to you: Reach out to God and have your own personal time with him. Tell him your problems, your fears, the uncertainties that flood your mind, and then wait to hear his response by reading his Word and seeking godly guidance. One of the hardest things to do is wait for God's timing. How will you know when it is God's time? Friend, everything will be in place because we serve a God who does not tolerate confusion. When you rush in front of God's will, things will not end the way you want them to.

That, my friend, is your gift for today.

The Guiding Hand

What does fifty-five years look like to you?
Does it seem ancient?
Molded and shriveled?
Is it just a number
That signifies a turn of the century?
Fifty-five years is time that has been led by the
Guiding Hand.
What does fifty-five years mean to you?
Does it signify determination?
How about resilience?
Is it just another big number
In the grand scheme of things,
A time etched in history?
Fifty-five years is time that has been led by the
Guiding Hand.
What does fifty-five years look like to you?
Does it seem nostalgic
As you hear accounts of a time
That seems just like old wives' tales:
Women in skirts and dress,
Men in woolen suits and bowler hats?
Is it a time so far removed from our jeans and flip-flops?
Fifty-five years is time that has been led by the
Guiding Hand.
What is fifty-five years to you?

Is it a time of reflection?
Or do you still bask in the limelight of the past?
Is it a time to wish for what we had,
A time to click our tongues and look confused,
Measuring our past accomplishments
To the challenges of today?
Fifty-five years is a time that has been led by the
Guiding Hand.
What does fifty-five years going forward look
like to you?
Definitely not time to sit on the laurels of the past.
Not the time to bask in yesterday's glow.
This is a time
To search deep within ourselves,
Deciding to stay the course for some;
Others need to get plugged in,
Get vested in our investment.
The next fifty-five years will still be led by the Guiding
Hand of God.
Fifty-five years!
Reflect…Yes.
See how far we have come. Yes.
Celebrate. Yes.
Reflect again. Yes.
Compare yesterday to today…No.
Step up to do your part. Yes.
Going forward,
What mark will you leave here?
As the next fifty-five is led by the Guiding Hand?
What will be said in the next fifty-five
When our future selves reminisce as we do today?

What stamp will you leave in the next fifty-five years?
Whom did you lead to Christ?
What influences did you create?
How faithful were you to the kingdom?
Only you can determine your mark
If you pray, stay faithful and encouraged,
And allow yourself to be guided by the Almighty hand.
The next fifty-five will point others to Christ,
Guided by the mighty hand of God.

Unwrapping the Gift

Strength for Today

For you have need of endurance, so that when you have done the will of God you may receive what is promised.

~ Hebrews 10:36

Imagine, you wake up and from start to finish, you do not have to worry about what you will eat, drink, or do. Everything is done for you, and most importantly, you trust all the decisions that are made for you. Can you imagine that life? Of course not because then you would have to be a robot or someone who has been hypnotized.

Are you guided? What or who guides you? When I see the shambles that people make of their lives, I start wondering what they have as a compass. Having a compass to guide us means that you are consulting it to take you through. A compass is used to ensure a person reaches their destination. That is what the presence of God does in our lives.

I wrote this piece when my church, Washington Shores Church of Christ, celebrated fifty-five years of God's faithfulness as we honored him on our church anniversary. Some might look at fifty-five years as a long time, and it is; however, it was a day to remember all who have contributed to the work of the church and to bless God with our praise for all he had seen us through and to hand ourselves over to him to take us through the years to come.

Do you reminisce on your life? What have you endured? How were you able to endure all you have been through? Was it by your own might, power, wealth, knowledge, and intellect?

My gift to you: Today, I encourage you to realize that what you have endured could only have been possible through the mighty power of God, and the only reason you were able to overcome is because of God. Having a grateful heart and making those praises known to others is what God Almighty desires from us. Giving God praise and sharing the love of God's guidance is a testimony that points others to Christ, and so we must continuously testify of God's goodness.

That, my friend, is your gift for today.

Part 5
The Gift of Provision

Photo credit: D.E.E.

Peace is conceived when your surrender comes in contact with God's mercy.

When God Provides

We ask.
Then we wonder,
Shocked,
Amazed,
When God provides.
We cry.
Scalding tears,
Salty and Unrestrained,
Then display disbelief
When God provides.
We rant.
We sure do rave!
We seem to be losing
Our simple minds.
But then we cannot believe
God has provided.
Why ask
But do not believe?
We doubt.
We do not rely.
But still we expect
For God to provide.
Yes.
This is about us.
You and me.

We should give thanks,
Share the good news with others,
Attest to his goodness
As God provides.
So we should smile,
Laugh, and shed tears of joy,
Rolling unrestrained down our faces,
Grateful that God has answered,
God has provided.

Unwrapping the Gift

Strength for Today

If you are willing and obedient, you shall eat the good of the land.

~ Isaiah 1:19

I am ever so baffled when I ask God to answer favorably my request and then when he does, I will always say; I just cannot believe this has happened! Why did I ask if I did not believe it would be fulfilled? So many of us are in this same situation where we ask but we really do not trust that our request will be made known to God and that he will supply all of our needs according to his will.

It is all about faith. We say we have a big God but with our feeble, earthly minds, we do not trust him until our requests are answered, and that is why we just cannot believe it has happened. Trust is the firm belief in the reliability, truth, ability, or strength of someone or something. We have to believe that not only will God answer our prayer with either yes, no, not now, or even never, but he will take care of us if we put ourselves into his hands for safekeeping.

When we take our money to the bank, we trust them to take care of it till we need it. When we make our requests known to the Lord, we say we believe and trust, but we hold our breath, waiting to see what will happen before we believe and trust. That is not the way to live.

My gift to you: When you ask God to see to your need, trust and believe that he will and can do it. After your need has been supplied, make sure you tell someone so that God gets the glory. Sometimes, you do not get what you ask for, and later on you realize that God, in his mercy, shielded you from yourself. If you have not testified to God's goodness towards you, you have not given him the glory. If you do not tell someone of God's goodness to you, you have not given him the praise. God asks us to trust him and that is all it requires…TRUST.

That, my friend, is your gift for today.

No Turning Back

I see you have come back
Again.
Even though you have been told
The welcome mat has been removed.
Still,
You return to try and grab a hold,
To insert yourself
Back
Into my life.
To reinstate our former relationship.
That former life is no more.
The chains you clamped on so tightly
Have been melted.
The person you see standing here before you
Has found a new love.
This love does not ensnare.
This new love does not enslave.
This love is beyond even my own comprehension.
This new love
Laid down his life.
His life, yes,
For me!
So, old partner
Why should I trade freedom for slavery?
Why choose shackles over liberty?

I have tasted goodness.
I have felt mercy.
I am enjoying mercy.
I am embracing who I am:
A princess in the courts of a King.
Daughter of a King.
I am embracing greatness.
This time,
I have no desire to return
To your clutches,
To the life of hopelessness and darkness.
No turning back.
No turning back.

Unwrapping the Gift

Strength for Today

"And God is able to make all grace abound to you,
so that having all sufficiency in all things at all
times, you may abound in every good work. As it is
written, '"He has distributed freely, he has given
to the poor; his righteousness endures forever."' He
who supplies seed to the sower and bread for food
will supply and multiply your seed for sowing and
increase the harvest of your righteousness."

~ 2 Corinthians 9:8–10

I remember the days of carefree living and "enjoying life." I hung out with my friends, went to parties, hosted parties, and thought all we were doing was enjoying the "spice of life." I now realize that I did not even know what life was back then. One day I collided with kindness and grace beyond any I could have ever conjured, and I fell to my knees and allowed my Savior to begin the work he had started years ago at my birth.

I have often watched documentaries where people say they have no regrets in their lives. They say if they could live life all over, they would do everything the same way. They always add that they would do everything the same way because of the outcome of where they are presently in their lives. I always feel a bit sad when someone says that we all should have regrets because we have not always been kind. Are we kinder today? Yes, we are, but remember, we might have scared someone with an unkind word. I regret that. Have we treated people poorly? Probably we have. And do we know what damage we cause? I regret those times in my life. Have we disregarded someone's feelings and love? I know I have, and I regret not handling things differently. I regret that.

As a daughter of the Most High God, I can look back and see that what I thought was freedom was actually slavery to sin. I saw myself running with the crowd, and sometimes the crowd ran over me and I just got back up and kept running with them. I had bruises and broken bones from all the activities until one day I realized I had to stop hurting myself and broke down to relinquish my life into the mighty hand of God the Almighty.

I am a much better human being today than I was the first thirty years of my life. I regret not being kinder, more loving, friendlier, understanding, empathetic, and sympathetic. We all know we cannot go back and undo the things we have done or failed to do in the past, but we can move forward in our future and with those past regrets planted firmly in our minds, live a much better life.

My gift to you: I cannot undo the unthinkable mistakes made in my past, but I can certainly move forward to do better with the rest of my life. I am not living in regret because that is detrimental. However, I am acknowledging that I can live harmoniously with my fellow man. I can treat others with the dignity and respect their humanity deserves.

My gift to you: Are you battered? Has life chomped on you and chewed you like tobacco and you are now rolled up in a ball and life is about to spit you into the gutter? Are you tired of forging your own life? Has what you have been doing worked for you? Are you succeeding? If you are like the person I used to be, you should be tired of running all day long. I hold a verse very dear to my heart, and it says, "Come to me all you who are weary and burdened, and I will give you rest." (Matthew 11:28). God wants to take away your troubles and give you the peace you need to lie contently in him. If you do not learn self-love in Christ, you will need repairs in your life. You have to willingly place your life in God's keeping to get rest and direction.

That, my friend, is your gift for today.

Lumley Beach

Seagulls
Chuckling,
Informing each other
Of the best sites to fish.
Waves crashing,
Bringing tidings
From exotic places.
Urchins and crabs
Scamper along
Gossiping about
This or that.
I am sitting
In the sand,
Toes deep,
Mind soaring.
This is my favorite spot,
My favorite place to read.
Lumley Beach.

Unwrapping the Gift

Strength for Today

But they who wait for the Lord shall renew their strength; they shall mount up with wings like eagles; they shall run and not be weary; they shall walk and not faint.

~ Isaiah 40:31

To this day, my favorite place to think and just be at one with nature is the beach. I see so much of God there that I have used its sands to walk away the aches of my day. I have used its waters as the waves come through to reassess my thoughts. I have used the unreachable horizontal ending to see how far my own dreams and aspirations can reach. I have looked up at the clouds to see the power and clarity that exists when I hand myself into the care of the One who created it all.

There is a peace when we find ourselves in places where we can be one with nature and just be ourselves.

My gift to you: Wherever you find peace, let that be the place you can always go back to. Sometimes it is not even a physical place you can go to but a place in your mind where you can commune with God and allow him to give you direction. If you have ever traveled a winding road overlooking a steep drop, you soon realize how perilous it is. That is what life can be likened to. When the driver is going at twenty-five miles per hour and you decide they are going too slow and you decide to take control and accelerate to one-hundred miles per hour, you will soon lose control and possibly cause a hurt that will be with you for the rest of your life. Lean back and allow God to take you through life because then you can be certain to get where you need to go and most importantly, get there in one piece.

That, my friend, is your gift for today.

The Giver Reclaims His Light

Today I heard
That the Lord sent his angel
To reclaim one of his own,
Taking back the luminance.
He loaned us for a little while.
The Giver has taken
His light back to its base.
Today my tears roll free
As a shadow passed
Over my weeping soul,
Deep, wrenching cries
Extracted from my innermost.
I dare not ask The Giver why.
I only know
We had a bright light
On loan to us,
Only for a little while.
Today I cried some more,
The light
That shone so bright
Through your smile
Has been extinguished,
Taken by the One
Who gave it to us.
"Only for a little while," he whispered.

Yes, today my heart truly hurts.
Today, I wonder
How grand it must be
For the Lord to hold you in his hand,
To be the one
Who helps illuminate the halls of gold.
How the jasper gleams
When your light flashes across.
Welcome! His open arms beckon
As you rest your head upon his bosom,
All weariness gone.
Today, I cried again.
We have suffered a great loss
Down here on earth,
But the Giver who gave
Has his light back at home.
It shines bright.
It shines.
Shines.
Singing "Amazing Grace."
Grace is amazing.
Today, through these tears
I say fare thee well, my dear,
We will not forget.
The Giver took one and left two.
As I look into the future,
I know I will see your brilliant smile
Shinning infectiously
On the faces of the Giver's gifts.
Today, I cried again.
The Giver took a small light.

He needed it somehow.
The one who gives
Has decided to take again.
Blessed be the name of the Lord.
We will remember
Your smile we will remember.
We will always remember
Our grace.
Today, I hurt again.
I am trusting solely on you.
The Giver
Who gives only perfect gifts?
Surely there is a reason
Though we do not understand
Here on earth.
The Giver asks
That we trust.
Trust.
Depend on and look only to him;
On him.
We fix our eyes on the Giver.
We will understand all this better
Tomorrow.
Today, I hurt.
My tears flow freely,
Unfettered.
I let my emotions go.
I shake uncontrollably,
Letting it all go.
Then, I feel your comfort
Reach from inside me.

165

You surround me with your love.
You lift my chin up to the heavens.
My tear-filled eyes behold a beautiful sight;
You and the children
Held tightly in God's bosom,
Shinning as the jewels on the jasper wall
Illuminated by your faces.
Today, I hurt.
Today, I find comfort.

Unwrapping the Gift

Strength for Today

May you be strengthened with all power, according to his glorious might, for all endurance and patience with joy.

~ Colossians 1:11

I can still remember the first time I met Maria Grace Miller. She read a poem at church and because I love poetry, I went up to her and told her she had talent and that I enjoyed her poem. One thing you notice about Maria is her beautiful, genuine smile that radiates like the sunshine.

Fast-forward years later, she and I grew close as friends and share a passion for education, mentoring young women, the African-American community and its issues, and activism.

I was in Sierra Leone when the sad news reached me that Maria had passed away. She was later laid to rest with her twin boys. Each day, The Giver reclaims a loaner but gives back hope. I could see God's love through this very painful time in the lives of Maria's family, and I could also feel God's love for us.

My gift to you: I have always wondered how people can bear to smile when they are going through seemingly unbearable pain. Even though the Christian endures the same pain as an unbeliever, the Christian holds onto the word of God. Sometimes you might want to scream and curl up in a tight ball, holding all the pent-up anger and frustration at a God you thought would answer your cries for healing. I have realized that it is not a test of your faith to cry and to scream and to roll up in frustration because you hurt. God knows your pain. Cry, scream, and reach out to open the word of God, where he has assured us that this is not our home.

Those who die in the Lord are with him. We can be assured that one day, we too will be with our loved ones. We are all destined to die, and we will miss our loved ones, and now after all the crying and sorrow, it is time to let our light shine to show the world that we serve a God who loaned us our family members. He has gone to prepare a place for us and where he is, there we too will be. We cling to that hope; those comforting words.

That, my friend, is your gift for today.

Thirty Five Thousand Feet

Shaking
Frightened
Can hardly breathe
Armrest clutched tightly
Head thrown back
Hyperventilating
I am about to lose my simple mind.
Then suddenly I remember
Even at ten thousand feet
You are here.
Doubtful
Regretful
Why did I forget?
When have you ever let go?
When have you not been enough?
When have you not held my hand?
Even at ten thousand feet
You are here.
Calm
Trusting
Protected
Your unseen hand has me,
Nestled oh so closely
In your care.
Feeling your warmth

Calms me.
Even at ten thousand feet
You are here.
Stronger
Peaceful
Tranquil
Blessed Assurance
I will never leave you nor forsake
Why worry?
Closer to the heavens
At ten thousand feet.
You have been here all along.

~ * ~

Unwrapping the Gift

Strength for Today

Blessed is he whose help is the God of Jacob, whose hope is in the Lord his God, who made heaven and earth, the sea, and all that is in them, who keeps faith forever; who executes justice for the oppressed, who gives food to the hungry. The Lord sets the prisoners free; the Lord opens the eyes of the blind. The Lord lifts up those who are bowed down; the Lord loves the righteous. The Lord watches over the sojourners; he upholds the widow and the fatherless, but the way of the wicked he brings to ruin.

~ Psalm 146:5–9

I hate flying! I once saw a plane crash at takeoff, and that sight always comes to my mind when I am in a plane and we are taking off. Every time I have to travel I feel as if I am walking the plank. I am deathly afraid, especially at takeoff when the plane accelerates, and I am almost flat on my back and gripping the armrest like a lifeline. Usually on my travels I am with my husband, who will ease my grip and hold my hand and rub the back of my hand in soothing strokes till my heart eases to its natural rhythm.

It was during a long flight to San Francisco that this poem was born. We had just lost my sister-in-law, and I was on my way to join my husband, who had been with her for about six weeks prior to her passing away. I was heartbroken and sad that she was no longer with us, and I was also feeling the loss of not having the comfort of my husband by my side when suddenly I remembered the Bible verses that God had given to help me to endure any situation. I reached and clung onto one of my favorites.

I was feeling scared and alone. The flight was going to be a long one and thankfully, I was alone in my row and had the presence of the Lord to engulf me. I began to talk to myself, telling my mind to be steadfast and trust in the Lord.

"You will keep in perfect peace those whose minds are steadfast, because they trust in you" (Isaiah 26:3).

My gift to you: There is nothing that is in your control. You can only control how you react to the situations that occur, and that is where you have power. That is also the place where you come face-to-face with the reality of who you are as a person under stress. When situations occur in your life that is when you collide with your weakness.

Your best option is to leave your life in God's care and then you do not have to worry about your life. He has control of everything.

God will keep in perfect peace a person whose mind is stayed and focused on him and him alone. As frail humans, we say we give our troubles to God, but normally we keep worrying until we get the satisfaction we crave. If you want peace, then leave it completely. Whenever you want to take it back up simply say to yourself, "God, I have already given it up to you, and I trust you to deal with this issue." Trusting God is the key to finding perfect peace.

That, my friend, is your gift for today.

Awesome God

We often wonder
Where God is.
We often doubt
If he even exists.
We take his mercy,
Dash it in the wake of our unfaithfulness.
We are ungrateful for his grace.
We show this
Through our callous worship.
We are not reverent,
Yet we bask in his glory
As his majesty is displayed
Through the signs of his wonder
Which all behold,
Wretched children that we are.
We must show our love
In the daily walk of our lives.
Our very lives should be
A living testimony
Of this great and awesome God
Who beholds the pillar of clouds above,
Who has fashioned
Every facet of our lives.
Who could be mightier than God?
His awesomeness

I cannot explain
But to see it
In the changing of the seasons,
The rising and setting of the sun,
The cycles of the moon,
The turning of the tide,
The birth of the young,
The rebirth of souls
Turning away from former things,
To walk
In the newness of life.
Who can explain
The awesomeness of God?
We use it, and we marvel
When we should
Bow down and adore him.
I cannot explain
The awesomeness of God.
All I can do
Is bow down and worship.

Unwrapping the Gift

Strength for Today

My God, my rock, in whom I take refuge, my shield, and the horn of my salvation, my stronghold and my refuge, my savior; you save me from violence. I call upon the Lord, who is worthy to be praised, and I am saved from my enemies.

~ 2 Samuel 22:3–4

One of my favorite things to do for myself is filling a tub with hot water, adding Epsom salts, one of Dr. Teals Foaming Baths, and a bath bomb. Then I soothe my body and soul by sitting in it and allowing those healing agents to pamper my body. I normally sit in that water for about an hour and while I am in the bath, I talk to God. I praise him for being my Lord and Savior, and I praise him for being awesome.

I also have a candle burning and soft music playing. I lean back and allow my mind to be in a state of calm and gratitude. I am always in that state of peace so that I never forget the blessings of what I have. I take the time to confess my shortcomings and praise him for all he bestows.

My gift to you: God has given us so much, and one way to repay him for what he does is to tell others about God's goodness so that others learn to trust in him too.

Our testimony is our words of praise. Being grateful is appreciating what you have been given.

That, my friend, is your gift for today.

Saved by Grace and Grace Alone

I was drowning,
Sucked into the mire
Of my own sin.
My life was being choked
Out of me
By deceit and depression.
They told me lies;
Being good was all it takes;
Showing kindness and giving alms,
Choking the life out of me,
Shrouding my eyes
With the cloak of indifference.
I was drowning.
Life slowly slipped away
By the hands of my own sin.
Then, you came.
You peeled away the scales.
Now I could clearly see
The quicksand of death.
I struggled to break free.
Patiently, you removed the fetters.
My arms swung wide as I reached for you,
Embracing your word and your love.
My body trembled in realization
That I could have died.

How close to the pit of Hades,
How near I was to eternal damnation.
You made me see myself
The way I really was.
I backed up into your arms;
Your arms of love and security,
A newness of life,
To be made new.
I shudder, just thinking
I was suicidal in my former life,
Dying by my own hands.
Then, you saved me,
Sharing freely with me
Your amazing grace.
Oh that blessed assurance
That now, since my change,
You are mine.
I will live abundantly in you.
I will be secure in you,
Covered with your protection
From now through eternity.
That is great news!

Unwrapping the Gift

Strength for Today

Let us hold unswervingly to the hope we profess,
for he who promised is faithful.

~ Hebrews 10:23

Have you ever felt like you were way over your head in a situation? Did it feel like you were drowning? I have been there, and I knew I was in trouble. I did not know what to do to save myself, but I had been given a gift as a child. My parents gave me the gift of knowing Christ and having him as the most integral part of my life. He saved me, and I am protected by God's love and his mercy and his grace.

My gift to you: You think that all hope is gone because of the deceit and the lies that seem to have choked the very life out of you. There is hope; there is always hope in Christ! You must cling to the word of God. He who promised…is faithful. Even though all around you there is chaos and strife, God has removed those fetters and all you have to do is be "unwavering" because regardless of all that is going on around your world…God is faithful. Each morning, God's grace reloads and is renewed with the opening of your eyes to a new day.

That, my friend, is your gift for today.

Tranquility

My favorite
Reading place is
On the beach
In the shade
Of a plush palm tree.
There I can bask,
Peace and quiet,
My mind in tune
With the place
I find myself,
That place we only go
In a good story.
There in the shade
Of that palm tree,
Not a care in the world
I can read
In tranquility.

Unwrapping the Gift

Strength for Today

May he grant you your heart's desire and fulfill all your plans!

~ Psalm 20:4

I love my peace. That space where I can just be at one with myself, my spirit, soul, and God. That is the epitome of tranquility. I am not thinking or stressing or wondering if things will go right. I am just still and completely at peace, knowing it is not in my hands and that everything will be all right. That is tranquility.

I could spend hours sitting at the beach, enjoying the soft breeze, tasting the salt in the air and the lulling of my spirit by the rolling waves. I love tranquility and peace, especially in nature where God's majesty is everywhere, and all I can do is shake my head in awe.

My gift to you: Have you ever gone to a store or tried to buy peace online? No one can sell you peace. Peace is conceived when your surrender comes in contact with God's mercy. Only God gives peace. When peace resides in you, there is no confusion and discord.

That, my friend, is your gift for today.

The City Awakens

Slowly, my eyes open
Adjusting to the dark.
The foul began to crow,
Sending the message
Like the beating of the talking drum:
Dawn is near!
Work must be done!
Resting time is over!
We must arise!
The city awakens.
Generators loudly humming,
Almost drowning out the sounds of dawn.
The sky's hues begin to lighten,
The layers peeled away by daylight
Darkness separating the hues of blue,
Gates creaking, opening and closing.
Preparation has begun.
The day must commence.
The city awakens.
(Morning in Freetown, Sierra Leone)

Unwrapping the Gift

Strength for Today

"For I know the plans I have for you," declares the Lord, "plans for welfare and not for evil, to give you a future and a hope."

~ Jeremiah 29:11

I love routines. That is what has made me successful. I know my alarm will alert me that it is 5:00 a.m. and time to get up out of bed (if I am not already up, which is most likely). I expect my alarm to also alert me that it is 5:20 a.m. and time to get dressed so that by 5:30 a.m., I'm well on my way to walk the seven miles that I trek each morning.

Today is different. I use the Map My Walk app and so I set it when I step off my driveway and onto the street to track my steps and miles. When I arrived at the 1-mile mark, I did not hear the expected voice of MMW. My thought was, maybe MMW could not override the music I was listening to, but she always interrupts to tell me where I am so I took out my phone and MMW was on pause. I am not sure what happened, but my first mile had not recorded.

My thoughts immediately went to despondency. We all tend to depend on things and people and when they fail us, the disappointment sometimes is crushing. My attitude was the same. I started thinking about what went wrong, and I did not follow my usual route because something had disrupted the flow of my walk, and I focused on that for most of my walk.

My gift to you: When something does not work out the way you have planned it, what do you do? Does it right itself because you are focused on the disappointment? You are eating yourself up with worry and stress, and has that helped make the situation any better? Of course the answer is no. Only God does not disappoint. You might have heard this before but I will say it again. "The man of this world will let you down but Jesus never fails."

That, my friend, is your gift for today.

Hilda: Bewilderment

News of you crashes the airways,
Our Lord has taken you away.
We are all shocked.
This is unbelievable!
Our Hilda is gone.
We find it difficult to believe
Our Lord hastily snatched you
Away from all you held dear.
We are stunned;
Our Hilda is gone.
We are weeping tears of disbelief.
Our lips tremble as we try to comprehend
This great loss of a loving spirit.
We are confused.
Our Hilda is gone.
We do not know what to say,
Neither do we know what to do.
Our mouths gape open,
We are speechless.
Our Hilda is gone.
Explaining our bewilderment
Would not sufficiently chronicle.
This is absolutely taken aback.
We are confused.
Our Hilda is gone.

Resolutely, we must surrender
To the one who gave,
Now decided to take away.
We are speechless.
"Alas, O Ayah!" This is the cry we make.
Our Hilda is gone.
(I will always miss you, Hilda Konteh)

Unwrapping the Gift

Strength for Today

Even though I walk through the valley of the shadow of death, I will fear no evil, for you are with me; your rod and your staff, they comfort me.

~ Psalm 23:4

I have had a lot of sorrow, which hits me so deeply sometimes; I find it difficult to breathe. In the midst of this turbulence is the thought of how incomplete my life would have been without the people God has reclaimed from my life.

One of the most heart-breaking losses I endured was the loss of Hilda. Hilda was my friend, and we had shared teenage fears and uncertainties and came out on the other side of adulthood. I had returned for the first time after eighteen years to my hometown of Freetown, Sierra Leone.

I remember sitting on the porch after taking a phone call when my sister came outside and asked if I had heard any news from America.

Usually when someone asks that question it is not good news they are asking about. She told me she heard that something unfortunate had happened to Hilda.

I called one of Hilda's relatives, and they confirmed that indeed Hilda had died the previous evening at her home. I was overcome with emotion, thinking back to the last time she had spent time with me when I visited my adoptive parents in Maryland.

My gift for today: Our precious loved ones might be gone from us in death, but having them in our life is still better than if we had never had them. Can you imagine how incomplete your life would have been without the loved one you are thinking about right now? Think of spending time with this person and then take them out of the picture like you never knew them, and see how incomplete the story is. Do not feel shame or apologize for crying or mourning visibly. There is power in mourning because it reveals the love you shared with another human.

That, my friend, is your gift for today.

Part 6
The Gift of Family

Family are the ones who take you into their hearts, love you and care for you, and they are there beside you crying with you when you hurt, laughing in your joy, concerned through your trials, and loving you through it all. If you have someone you call family, you have wealth beyond measure.

The Unit

My family: the unit
Is like a chicken casserole dish.
Each member of the unit
Brings a distinct contribution.
Each of us is the part of the chicken you like;
Without this main ingredient,
The casserole loses its identity.
Each member of the unit
Brings a special feature
Unique to them
Essential for the unit.
My older sisters are the stock;
The base liquid
Needed before the dish is prepared.
My older brothers are the onion,
Adding much-needed flavor.
Too much and you become uncomfortable.
My other sister is like the yellow bell peppers
Much needed in the dish,
Adding color to the casserole.
Without all of these, the dish would not be called
A chicken casserole dish.
The delicious meal.
My family is like a casserole.
It takes many ingredients

For it to turn
Into a delicious meal.
My family: the unit
Is like a chicken casserole dish.
The more we work together,
The better we all become.
My Family
The Unit

Unwrapping the Gift

Strength for Today

*For everything there is a season, and a time for
every matter under heaven: a time to be born, and
a time to die; a time to plant, and a time to pluck
up what is planted.*

~ Ecclesiastes 3:1–2

So many of us have been gifted with family members
who have been given to us by God the Father. Someone
once said, "You do not pick your family members; you are
placed in a family by God." Sometimes family members can
be your worst enemies because of one reason or another;
jealousy, envy, family strife, and dissension. Whatever the
reasons why your family is united or divided, you have a
choice to make. You can either allow them to steal your

joy by being drawn into their drama or love them from a distance.

When God placed us in our families, he had a great plan far beyond us to comprehend. One thing I do know is that no one is beyond God's grace and mercy. I do not know your particular issue with your family, but I do know that God will give you a way out if you seek his will.

Personally, I have made peace with my own family. I love each and every one of them but it was a painful, agonizing, excruciatingly long road to realize and accept that some will never love and care for me the way I love and care for them. I also have come to the painful realization that because I have shielded them from the world by not revealing their mistakes and flaws, that doesn't mean they will do the same for me. It is a hard lesson to learn that not all of your family members will jump puddles for you even though you have jumped oceans for them.

God is faithful, and he will place others in your life to fill the void. We belong to a bigger family than those we share bloodlines with.

My gift to you: The family of God within the Christian Church is also our family, and these are the people with whom we will share eternity in the heavenly realm. Remember, we are not perfect as Christians, but we share a love given to us by Christ Jesus. God, in his great wisdom, has not left us without a way out. The goal should always be to dwell in heaven with our lord and savior Jesus Christ with our family, the family of God.

That, my friend, is your gift for today.

Ode to My Father: Papa

I still see you,
Impressionistic and strong
Strength of the alpha man
Significant in all his glory.
I see you still, my father: Papa,
Virile and robust,
Revolutionary in leadership and thought.
I see you, my father: Papa,
Scholarly and ambitious
Symbolic of so many
Born before their time.
I see you still, my father: Papa,
Stalwart and spirited,
Immaculately dressed in white.
I still see you, my father: Papa,
Astute and observant,
A visionary, an intellectual.
I still see you, my father: Papa,
Ingenious and shrewd,
A businessman.
I still see you, my father: Papa,
Adept and dapper,
Muscular and winsome.
I still see you, my father: Papa,
Observant and strapping,

Debonair and always congenial.
I still see my father: Papa.
Papa, I see you.

Unwrapping the Gift

Strength for Today

As a mother comforts her child, so will I comfort you; and you will be comforted over Jerusalem.

~ Isaiah 66:13

My father's presence was always felt in our home. We constantly would hear the words, "Wait till your father gets home." If it was a disappointing report card, we would tell our mother the details, but it was opened only when our father returned home. If it was misplaced behavior, it was handled effectively when Papa came home, even though Mama personally took care of some issues as well.

We respected our father. He provided for us and taught us how to own up to our errant actions. As a teenager, he would sit me down and warn me of "sweet words" spoken by boys. He assured me that no man would ever love me as much as he did and that I should not be swayed by "sweet words" such as, "your lips are as beautiful as a flower, your lips are as rosy as a rose, and you are my sunshine."

My father always told me I was beautiful, and he warned me of nonsensical words boys and young men would say to me just to have their way with me. Even as an adult, whenever the opposite sex gives me a compliment, I think of my father's warnings.

I am not sure whether you have a relationship with your father or if you even know him. I can tell you that regardless of the relationship or lack thereof with your earthly father, we have a Heavenly Father who is the ultimate father. I can count the many times my earthly father failed me, even though he was a great father, but not a single time has God my Heavenly Father ever let me down.

My gift to you: God has given me the greatest gift— Jesus Christ and a peace that surpasses all I could ever hope for or dream of. You also have the same Heavenly Father that I have. He will make a way when all roads seem closed. He will provide. He will heal. In his mercy, he will take away, and he will never leave you. He will come when you call; he hears when you pray. He will grant you your needs and when you trust him, he will guide you over the mountains and through the valleys of this life. When you accept your Heavenly Father, you will begin to resemble him. Soon, others will see his likeness reflected through you. Our task is to point others to our Heavenly Father.

That, my friend, is your gift for today.

Ode to Mama

How can I eulogize you?
What could I possibly say
That would epitomize
The very essence of you?
What could I possibly say to praise you?
For raising so many children;
Distinctions—I never saw
Of yours, mine, and ours
Till cruelty peeled the innocent scales away.
Oh, Mama,
My heart is irreparably broken,
Fragmented into uncountable pieces,
Fragmented pieces that cry out.
Each piece cries out for your warmth.
My mind's eye still sees and feels you
Quietly sitting,
Observing
In your corner chair,
Analyzing, examining closely all activities,
Lending guidance where needed.
Oh, Mama,
I see you everywhere in my home.
Your presence lingers,
Filling the empty spaces;
The potted plants in the corners,

The backyard fruit trees and gazebo,
The patio with the dogs.
We all ache at this sudden loss.
Mama,
Oh, Mama,
When will my tear duct well dry up?
When will the burning ache in my heart,
The shards of fragmented pieces,
The longing in my soul,
Such a deep and jaggered wound,
How will this heart heal when each day another
cut ensues?
Mama,
How can I even begin to eulogize you?
Through my memories,
Your life shines bright.
My life will represent
A story that cannot be told
Merely through a eulogy.
What you taught and instilled
Will be the only eulogy that will be seen,
Not heard.

Unwrapping the Gift

Strength for Today

You, LORD, hear the desire of the afflicted; you encourage them, and you listen to their cry.

~ Psalm 10:17

A godly mother is an everlasting gift from God.
Heaven holds my blessed mother.
It is mind-boggling the value of the gifts God gives us.
Eighty-six years ago,
Heaven sent a gift to earth.
That gift was placed in a struggling home,
Raised by a single dad, and then a woman
Entered her life.
God sent a gift; that gift had a rough start.
That gift.
The gift married.
That gift.
The gift received other gifts
Just like she had been a gift
So many years earlier.
This is a season when
Most people give gifts
And people show appreciation.
You might not appreciate
The blessings of gifts

The Lord has given.
I am grateful for the gift of my mother
And I know that if God had not given her to my family,
Our lives might have taken a different turn.
Heaven, you hold my blessed mother.
You hold my mother in your tender care.
Thank you.

My gift to you: A godly mother is an everlasting gift from God. If you have a mother who rebukes you and uses God's Word to help convict you of the wrongs you are doing, and if she is not scared to tell you to your face that you need to turn to the Lord, you have a godly mother. A mother who is unyielding, who always points her children to God's mercy seat is a gift that will keep on giving through the training she instilled in her children.

That, my friend, is your gift for today.

Gratitude for Mama

The deep longing for you remains,
Even though it has been six years today.
The unexplained, aching pain of loss,
My head resting on your headstone moss
Has dulled to a nagging pain
Coursing through my veins.
Awakens a desire so deep,
Rising my emotions into weeping.
Even though you reside in heaven
I am saddened by your leaving;
God took you too soon
After you saw the light that afternoon.
Today and always
Gratitude and love
Will always be my theme
For encouraging my dreams,
Praying for all your children.
I thank God for you, Mama,
This day and always.
Thank you, Lord, for my mother.

Unwrapping the Gift

Strength for Today

He heals the brokenhearted and binds up their wounds.

~ Psalm 147:3

I can still recall the first recollection I have of my mother telling me she loved me. My wedding day. As a child, teenager, young adult, to womanhood, I never once doubted her love for me. As an African girl, I always felt both of my parents' love through the care they gave to all of us, yet it was refreshing to hear her utter the words which all of a sudden meant so much to me. Maybe it is because I was in my new country, the United States, and had become accustomed to hearing the words so often in this society where people look for validity and assurance.

So many times in our lives, we look to others to validate that we deserve what God has rightfully given to us. I have always been a person who prefers actions to words. My parents provided and gave the best they could as often as they could and that was sufficient for me at the time. I have come to realize that my parents gave what they had to give, which was all of themselves, with the knowledge that they had. I know that neither of my parents' own parents ever told them they loved them, but they knew it.

My gift to you: I pray that today, you can look yourself in the mirror and know that beyond a shadow of a doubt you are loved by God. He showed his love in such a vivid portrayal that no one on this earth could ever refute it. Christ died for us all. God's love is all we need, and if that is not love, what is? Be blessed!

That, my friend, is your gift for today.

As I Watched

As I watched you slowly slip away
My mind reflects to that other time
Not too long ago
When another beloved soul
Was recalled to its Owner as the light beckoned.
Tears cascaded down my face
As I watched you slowly slip away.
As I watched you slowly slip away
I was reminded that this body
We take such good care of is but a shell
That houses our "real self."
This outer covering is a
Shelter for our imperishable, accountable soul.
As I watched you slowly slip away,
As I watched you lying there,
Sound asleep without a care,
My view was clouded by the haze of tears.
I grabbed and held onto the closest person;
A tight grip. I wanted to hold you back!
But you had already taken flight,
Returned to the Maker who sent you here.
As I watched you lying there,
As I poured out my grief,
I was reminded that
"We have no abiding city here."

I hang onto the ultimate reassurance that
"To be absent from the body is to be present with
the Lord."
The pain of your return to the Lord cuts deep,
A reminder that even as we watch
The Lord's will…will be done.
RIP Bill… "My Real Man"

Unwrapping the Gift

Strength for Today

*You, LORD, hear the desire of the afflicted; you
encourage them, and you listen to their cry.*

~ Psalm 10:17

My brother-in-law was very special to me. He was the first person to welcome me into the Ellis family before Phil even thought about proposing. He told me I would be his sister-in-law and that he was keeping me because I would be "good" for his brother. Then he began to demand that I pay a fee for the name after we got married. I always had a comeback for him though but always felt loved and accepted and appreciated.

To see him lying in that hospital bed so strong, vital, and looking so alive, I felt a pain so deep as I gazed into his hazel eyes that stared lifelessly at me. I remember placing my hand over his eyes to close them and kissed his forehead. I cried in anguish, but I knew that he would not have liked to be sick in a bed in a hospital.

Family is one of the greatest gifts God gave us.

My gift to you: We have all heard the advice, "Treasure your family," and today I also share that greatest of advice with you. Our family might not be as wonderful as other families, or have money or status, but one thing I can give you is that family are the ones who take you into their hearts, love you and care for you, and they are there beside you crying with you when you hurt, laughing in your joy, concerned through your trials, and loving you through it all. Let us not wait for family reunions, weddings, graduations, and death to help open our eyes to the fragility of our family. If you have someone you call family, you have wealth beyond measure.

That, my friend, is your gift for today.

Second Time Around

Second time around,
The cold room,
Crisp sheets
Antiseptic odors fragrance the air,
The poking and prodding,
Needles unearthing veins
Hiding in fear of discovery.
I lay calm and serene,
Knowing I rest comfortably in you.
The bed moves on silent wheels
To the short destination.
Smiling faces over me
Determined to calm my spirit.
Explanations long told
Before this moment
Now resound through my mind.
I rest peacefully
Knowing you are holding my hand.
I awake…slowly.
Shallow pain.
Dry throat and mouth.
Was this another aborted venture?
The reassuring smiles tell all.
It was tedious, but successful.
My insides are straightened out.

I am relieved.
Finally, the fight is over,
Reassured you are with me...always.
Four days laid up,
Unable to remove my gaze from you
I share my gratitude with others,
A testimony of your goodness.
A declaration of your mercy.
A testament of your love.
Undeserved, but a much-needed love.

Unwrapping the Gift

Strength for Today

A devout man who feared God with all his house-hold, gave alms generously to the people, and prayed continually to God.

~ Acts 10:2

Have you ever received a second chance? Your parents gave you grace for something you should clearly have received a punishment you would never forget, but they gave you leniency. Your boss gave you another chance even though you had been warned. You forgave yourself for not listening to your inner self and after much prayer, you gave yourself another chance to learn...to love.

I had been taken into surgery but had to be sewn back up because my surgeons saw something they needed to investigate further (Scar Tissue). I saw this second opportunity as a second chance to have things corrected. It was a chance also for me to understand God's grace and healing power. I have been a Christian for a long time, but during this time of uncertainty, I had the opportunity to clear my mind and hand my life over to him so he could be in complete control. That surgery was a turning point in my life. God became very real to me.

My gift to you: We must realize that God does not want parts of our lives. God wants it all. When we hand our lives over to Christ, he is the driving force, and we do not need to worry about where he is leading because he will lead us where we need to go and where we need to be.

That, my friend, is your gift for today.

Death: A Constant Reminder

It seems as if
Death is constantly
Knocking at our door.
Death seems to hover
Over our portal,
Shadowing our joy.
Even death's shadows
Are unrelenting in their pursuit,
Blindsiding us at every turn.
We ask for respite,
Our beaten shoulders droop,
Bowing low under our cares.
Death has revisited us
Time and time again.
We ask: When will you move on
And allow our hearts to mend?

Unwrapping the Gift

Strength for Today

But the steadfast love of the Lord is from ever-lasting to everlasting on those who fear him, and his righteousness to children's children, to those who keep his covenant and remember to do his commandments.

~ Psalm 103:17–18

I have given many hugs in sympathy when someone's loved one passes away. I have held hands and cried together with many friends and church family members. Others have hugged and held my own hand when first my beloved mother passed on to be with the Lord.

The pain is somewhat different. This pain was filled with amazement at how God does exactly what pleases him, and all we are left to do is to trust him fully for our every need.

A song was given me that reveals that the trials we endure on this earth are God's blessings in disguise.

I often wonder what God knows when he recalls our loved ones' souls back to himself. God, in his mercy, saw fit to take our loved ones.

Did God save my mother from a life of health concerns? I do not know what was on God's mind, but I do know that I hurt because of the physical separation, but I am assured that I will be reunited with her again one day on the beautiful shore.

My gift to you: Whatever your circumstances, be assured that God loves you, and if you trust him, he will see you through. Loss is a complicated feeling that no one can direct for you. Grief is personal, and as you mourn, just never forget that no amount of sorrowing will bring that person back, but the way you continue to live will bring that person's memory to light and many will benefit because they lived. Live their memory as a testimony, which will shed light on God's goodness that they lived.

That, my friend, is your gift for today.

Five Half-Inch Cuts

Spread out across my belly
Are five tiny cuts;
Reminding me of my frailty,
Reminding me of your grace,
Reminding me that this body is decaying daily.
Five tiny cuts;
A reminder that I must stay humble,
Constantly giving thanks;
These five tiny cuts
An everlasting reminder
To keep me on my knees
At times when I want to rise
Too quickly.
I will stay down
One moment longer
To give thanks
For the five tiny cuts
Created to save me,
This badge of remembrance,
A memorial to God's love and mercy.
Five tiny cuts.

Unwrapping the Gift

Strength for Today

Above all, keep loving one another earnestly, since love covers a multitude of sins.

~ 1 Peter 4:8

When something disappoints us, we often think of what we could have done differently to get another outcome. We experience hurt and then guilt and then regret because most times, we have seen the worst coming but we chose not to acknowledge it. I have learned over the years not to have regrets for allowing someone into my life. I have learned not to regret being kind or giving someone an opportunity when I have the upper hand.

Each time I look at the five half-inch cuts on my abdomen, I am reminded of God's grace. I could choose to view the scars as marks of imperfection, but all I see is an overwhelming gratitude that I survived. I proudly wear those five half-inch cuts, and I am proud to share them with the world whenever the opportunity presents itself.

My gift to you: Each time I see a surgery's reminder on my body, I am reminded of the fragility of the human body. We see ourselves sometimes as indestructible and almost bionic, since so many body parts can now have artificial replacements. God wants us to never forget that we have an origin, and one day, we will return to that from whence we came. Never forget that even though you might want to have a perfect and flawless body, one day, God will recall your soul, which is what your body enshrines. Be ready for the calling because when it is said and done, your soul will be required to give an account. Live well.

That, my friend, is your gift for today.

Just Seventeen

Who would have imagined
When you left home,
Taking a walk
To the corner store
To buy snacks and a drink,
You would never return
To the warmth and security
Of your home.
Just seventeen.
Who would have thought
That as you walked home,
Quietly talking on your phone
Through your family's community,
A legal stalker
Would follow you and snuff out your life
Like a candle extinguished by wind.
Your dad
Will never hug you again.
Just seventeen.
Who would have thought
The stalked
Would end up dead.
The stalker
Not guilty
Of carelessness and recklessness,

Of being the cause of your demise,
Of shooting you dead.
Just seventeen.
Who would have thought
In this great land of opportunities,
Where animals have rights and permanent habitats,
The black man
Still remains an endangered species.
Unfair laws
That make wrongs right,
Refusing to acknowledge the crime
In a young boy's death.
Just seventeen.
Who would have thought
You would be cast a villain
While your killer
Is hailed a victim,
Even though he still breathes.
In your grave,
Brought down by a cowardly bullet.
Just seventeen
While you lay cold.
Who would have thought
That our children are not safe
Even when we give them "The Talk."
They are profiled.
They are judged
By their varying shades of ebony,
And yes, the clothes they wear.
Dead.
Just seventeen.

Who would have thought
For the first time in my life,
Now I have a longing to acquire a weapon
To protect me and my children
Though I know
I would never kill another
Judging by hue or cloth.
You have brought this change in me
Even though I never knew you.
You have definitely made a difference in my life.
Just seventeen.
Who would have thought it?
This deep sadness we feel,
This shattering of our souls
At the callous accusations and portrayal,
The miscalculated prosecution,
Our lives changed forever.
Our children we must prepare
To face a cruel and biased world.
Just seventeen.
You were wronged,
But in your death
You have awakened the sleeping giant:
The awareness
To the plight of people of color.
You have become
A difference-maker.
Who would have thought
That at your death
We all learned valuable lessons?
Just seventeen

Yet you touched the whole world.
Rest in Perfect Peace, Trayvon

Unwrapping the Gift

Strength for Today

Love does no wrong to a neighbor; therefore love is the fulfilling of the law.

~ Romans 13:10

As I write this message geared to strengthening you, I am filled with extreme sadness for the young life so cruelly snuffed out in the callous killing of Trayvon Martin. For a long time, I hesitated to write this message because I had a son who was alive and well at the time Trayvon was killed. I too was deathly afraid of how my son would be perceived for standing up for his human rights and have that right taken away from him because someone "stood their ground." In actuality, the killer trampled on Trayvon's rights.

I do not know the parents or anyone affiliated with Trayvon, but as a mother, I feel their pain to this day. I often wonder what it would take to make people of power and privilege see our children as children instead of something to fear. What does it take to make a father look at a young man and think of his own son or daughter and not want to harm them? What would it take for one human to look at another human and see them for who they are…HUMAN.

As I write these words to strengthen you, it is 2020 and our world is in turmoil with the senseless killings of Trayvon Martin, Tamir Rice, Michael Brown, Eric Garner, Philando Castile, Breonna Taylor, and George Floyd (to name a very few). We as humans cannot stand aside and think the atrocities other races are enduring do not apply to us. We all have a moral duty to say something and do something by joining forces with civic organizations to help educate others to how, with our collective voices, we can join forces to get some laws changed. Changing of certain laws that currently protect perpetrators will ultimately lead to change.

My gift to you: We must be our brother's keeper. Many times we see a beggar, the homeless, or people of other races and because of their unfortunate situations, we think they are beneath us. In case you do not know, we are all created equal, even though some might be more fortunate than others. Being less fortunate is not a mark of unequal. Have compassion and speak out against the subtle or blatant racism in this world and then you can count yourself as one making a difference in the lives of others.

That, my friend, is your gift for today.

We Are Together Again

It has been a while;
Actually, it has been a long while
Since I have seen you.
Anticipating our reunion
Keeps me awake,
Wondering how it will be,
How I will feel,
Wondering, somehow,
If you would feel the same way too.
We have met;
The love overflows,
Swelling from our hearts,
Bursting through the tear ducts,
Flowing freely down our faces.
Anticipation has turned to jubilation.
We are finally here,
Giving and receiving love.
We cling together and cannot let go.
We are together once again.
(For Harriet)

Unwrapping the Gift

Strength for Today

And as you wish that others would do to you, do so to them.

~ Luke 6:31

One of my favorite people on this planet is my friend Harriet. She and I met when we both taught at the Annie Walsh Memorial School in Freetown, Sierra Leone. We grew into mature ladies, and we shared many secrets, and we gave each other sound advice as we lived life.

Some years ago, after being away from my country of birth, I returned for a visit and even though it had been over eighteen years since we separated, our reunion seemed as if we had not been separated for so many years; Harriet and I were together again.

I was amazed at how we just picked up our friendship where it had paused so many years before. One of my favorite memories was when she had helped me pack my suitcase when I left Freetown in 1996. She also came to pack my suitcase when I was returning to the United States in 2012.

My gift to you: When love is genuine, the roots are deep, and even though the storm of life can topple the tree, the roots are underground and hold securely the love begun so many years ago. True and genuine love does not fade away over time.

That, my friend, is your gift for today.

Sierra Leone
Salone

O Salone, my beautiful Salone,
With your white diamond glistening sands,
Majestic, proud mountains
Gazing ethereally upon the land.
Sunshine bright
Sparkling like a polished nugget
O Salone, my beautiful Salone,
From far and near they come
Lion mountains protector
Freetown…home to the free.
O Salone, my beautiful Salone,
Fishermen dragging nets, ready to sell.
Lush, green forests, roaming animals
Farming, palm wine, taping, mining
O Salone, my beautiful Salone,
Freetown, home of the free.
O Salone, my beautiful Salone,
Lion mountains ever keeping watch.
O Salone, my beautiful Salone
You forever hold my heart.

Unwrapping the Gift

Strength for Today

And hope does not put us to shame, because God's love has been poured into our hearts through the Holy Spirit who has been given to us.

~ Romans 5:5

I was born in Sierra Leone, West Africa, and it is a magical place that is deeply rooted in the arteries and veins of my heart. We have experienced civil unrest, yet the place of my birth remains a beautiful memory that will forever warm my heart.

I went back to Sierra Leone after being away for almost eighteen years. As the plane descended to the tarmac, I could feel the beat of the drums calling my name and beckoning me home. "Home is where the heart is." My heart is in the land of my birth. Every time I think of Sierra Leone, my heart warms up, and even though things have not been perfect for this rich land of my birth, I have a great appreciation for having a start in this land. Be grateful for where you call home.

My gift to you: We are living in our earthly home, but we have a much better place awaiting us faithful Christians when we transition from this world to our everlasting home to be with our Lord and Savior, Jesus

Christ. That is a place I look forward to residing in. As a Christian, I strive to live a life pleasing and worthy of a place in the heavenly choir to sing eternal praise to the Lamb of God. Each of us should hold onto the assurance that our Lord told his disciples before he went back to glory, "I go to prepare a place for you so where I am there you will be also" (John 14:3).

One day, we will be with the Lord for all eternity.

That, my friend, is your gift for today.

Part 7
Good Advice

Photo credit: D.E.E.

Each day, each of us has a golden opportunity to have a do-over. We can start over, walk away, think smarter, be positive, grieve less, and start to heal, soak longer in the tub, take a longer shower, and write that poem or first chapter of that book. Each day, we have opportunities to seize.

So…seize the opportunities today provides.

A Lesson Learned

When you do not learn the first time,
Other lessons will come to straighten you out.
Some lessons come to prepare us
For what is to come.
Some view lessons as stumbling blocks in their paths
Meant to block their way,
To derail them,
Meant to cause bodily harm.
Lessons are meant to teach,
To impart valuable lessons.
Some lessons can be used immediately.
Other times,
The application has to be stored away,
Brought to the forefront
To be recalled
At the opportune time.
Yes, a lesson is meant to be learned;
How it is applied
Depends solely on the learner.
To be correct,
The application of a lesson learned
Depends solely on the one who listens,
The person who did not merely
Sit passively through the lesson.
The learner allows the lesson

To sift and filter through their very soul.
The lesson is not to just pass through,
Shifting through the pores
Like quickly gulped water filters through the bladder.
The lesson should permeate
Through every fiber
So this learner has acquired knowledge.
When you do not learn the first time,
Other lessons will come to straighten you out.
The lessons of life,
The experiences of what others put us through,
This learner has learned:
The goal is attained,
Accomplished,
A lesson truly learned.

Unwrapping the Gift

Strength for Today

And without faith it is impossible to please him, for whoever would draw near to God must believe that he exists and that he rewards those who seek him.

~ Hebrews 11:6

Did you learn your lesson? My mother asked me that question after I had made a horrible mistake, and she wanted to know if I learned anything from that experience. So many times something happens to us and we do not slow down to analyze what happened, why it happened, and what we can get from the results of what happened.

Did you learn your lesson from that breakup? Did you learn your lesson from getting fired? Did you learn your lesson from that betrayal from someone you trusted? Did you learn your lesson when you moved to that area even though you were advised not to move there? Did you learn your lesson from...?

My gift to you: Everything that happens to us is a lesson to be learned. You must take a step back and learn from it so that you do not repeat the same mistake. You must look deeply at situations so you do better next time. Any lesson taught that you do not find something to learn from will cause you some pain or discomfort when you do not learn from it.

That, my friend, is your gift for today.

Finding the Balance

Trying to find the balance
Between parenthood and parenting,
Between upholding rules and standards
To understanding why my son
Always chooses to walk outside
The lines
Instead of within
The lines of the boundaries.
I wonder what benefits will come
From the hard knocks he receives
Each time he decides
To get off the chalk line.
I can only hope
And pray
That somehow, these lessons
Will make my boy
Into a productive man.

Unwrapping the Gift

Strength for Today

Let your reasonableness be known to everyone. The Lord is at hand; do not be anxious about anything, but in everything by prayer and supplication with thanksgiving let your requests be made known to God.

~ Philippians 4:5–6

Finding balance means you have been available for everyone around you, and you realize that you deserve time for yourself to just take care of you. Many times, we involve ourselves in so many things, and we tend to stretch ourselves very thin. We can work hard and be the one everyone runs to, but if we do not find time to balance it all with time to nourish ourselves – as we know when stretched too thin there tends to be a tear –the end result is never beneficial for anyone that is in our lives.

When we stretch ourselves too thin is when we say things to people that we want to take back but cannot. Other times, we indulge in harmful behaviors because of our inability to say no. We often want to please everyone and cannot really please anyone.

My gift to you: It is great to be the one who is on everyone's list when they need a shoulder to lean on or a sympathetic ear to listen. If you cannot give the same care to yourself, soon the ones you are helping will not have you to care for them. Finding the balance to care for oneself is a better example to show others how to care for themselves.

That, my friend, is your gift for today.

I Used To Wonder

I used to wonder
Why bad things happened
To great and faithful people.
I used to wonder
Just how these people felt:
If they still looked up to you,
If they still called on you
To see them through
All the calamities
They were undergoing.
I used to wonder
If those great and faithful people
Called out your name at night
During their midnight hour.
Did they cry out to you
As the Author and Finisher
Of their faith?
I used to wonder
Just how these people felt
When you came,
Many times without notice,
Not a hint to let them know
That you were ready
To take back what was yours,
To reclaim the soul

That you sent to them;
Only a loan
But they have loved it so dearly
They forgot that it had to be returned.
I used to wonder
How it actually felt
To realize it was only temporary;
This soul you gave
Was only theirs for a little while.
I used to wonder
Just how those people felt:
If they still looked up to you
With eyes trusting and dependent.
I used to wonder how it felt,
Till I became one of those people.

Unwrapping the Gift

Strength for Today

He will wipe away every tear from their eyes, and death shall be no more, neither shall there be mourning, nor crying, nor pain anymore, for the former things have passed away.

~ Revelation 21:4

When horrible things happened to people, I used to wonder how they felt. I am a very empathetic person, so I would try to stand in their shoes and ask my own self how I would feel if that situation happened to me.

I used to wonder this when I went to funerals and people were inconsolably weeping and it seemed as if their tear ducts were just pools of water because the tears just would not stop, and I would think later how they felt and when would they stop crying.

One day I had a loss, and now I do not need to wonder anymore. The pain is like none I have ever felt. It is like someone took a knife and cut you and each time you think of what happened to you, salt was poured and rubbed in the cut.

My gift to you: Your pain is valid. No one can ever feel your loss; in fact, no two people can grieve alike. Know that the pain you feel is because of the love you had for the person who is no longer with you. Cry and weep, and each time you think of your loved one, go out of your way to be kind to someone. Thinking and acting outside yourself and your pain will help you to heal your brokenness.

That, my friend, is your gift for today.

I Listened and I Learned: Through It All

What have I learned?
In the lifetime of this present life,
The teachings of my mother,
The instructions of my father,
The solid foundation of my upbringing,
Have taught me to look up,
To see you and you alone.
What have I learned?
I have learned that the words
Of my parents are true.
Seeking you with all my heart
Ensures that I remain
Within your perfect will,
Assurance that you will guide me.
What have I learned?
That if I remain faithful
You will carry me through.
You require my loyalty;
Loyalty to who I am,
Complete reliance in you.
My parents taught me;
I listened, and I learned.

Unwrapping the Gift

Strength for Today

For God gave us a spirit not of fear but of power and love and self-control.

~ 2 Timothy 1:7

We take for granted our upbringing, especially when what we have been taught collides with new teachings and knowledge. Immigrating to the United States opened my mind to so many aspects of child rearing, and at the same time, it put me at odds with my African upbringing, namely Sierra Leonean and specifically Martin and Matilda's teachings with the Holy Bible as a foundation backed up with tradition, and then their own perspectives.

Someone once said; If children came with a manual, we all would raise our children well. Children are different from one child to the next, so we cannot raise our children the same way. We must have standards and a baseline like: You must be respectful, not lie or steal, etc.

My parents were strict and structured. They believed in training the child in the way that they should go, and when they are older, they will not depart from it (Proverbs 22:6). Being in America and hearing parents asking their children for permission was very foreign to me, and seeing this gave me pause and appreciation for my strict parents.

Are there things they did that I would do differently? A definite yes. But am I grateful? A resounding yes.

Then I turn to the ultimate guide: The Holy Bible and what it says about the upbringing of children.

"Discipline your children, and they will give you peace of mind and will make your heart glad" (Proverbs 29:17).

My gift to you: I have come to realize that my parents knew a lot more than I gave them credit for. Parents are the roadmap to a bright future. They have already walked the road, and they want to help us go through it as well. Sometimes, parents just want us to walk where they have trod, but we need a compass to walk the walk. As the African proverb says, Children can walk fast down the path, but only a parent can lead them to their destination. Parents are the tour guides God gave to help children survive this world.

That, my friend, is your gift for today.

My Foundation Shaken: We Cling to You

We felt the earth move,
Shifting beneath us.
We felt it shake.
Trouble has shaken the base,
The foundation of our faith
Shaken.
Trouble is never far from the believer.
The testing of our faith,
Ensuring we maintain a childlike trust
That our fall has a cushion
Our hand will always be held,
Comforted.
We felt the earth shift beneath our feet;
Terrifying news
Bringing tears and a trembling heart.
The pain for the past.
We cry for you and remember our own loss.
Unbelievable.
Yes, the earth has shaken.
Our feet slip and slide,
But our foundation remains strong.
This news of our ultimate end
Has brought us to our knees.

Still, we cling to you.
(Our cheeks are still wet for Pa Temple.)

Unwrapping the Gift

Strength for Today

For everything there is a season, and a time for every matter under heaven: a time to be born, and a time to die; a time to plant, and a time to pluck up what is planted; a time to kill, and a time to heal; a time to break down, and a time to build up; a time to weep, and a time to laugh; a time to mourn, and a time to dance; a time to cast away stones, and a time to gather stones together; a time to embrace, and a time to refrain from embracing.

~ Ecclesiastes 3:1–17

When tragedy occurs suddenly and we have hardly had the opportunity to catch our breath, we are left bereft of breath, and it seems as if our head continues to reel as we wonder in disbelief.

I was in Sierra Leone when I received the sudden and abrupt news that my sister-in-law's father had passed away. It was Father's Day, and he had just returned from church when cardiac arrest stole his life away from all who loved him. We sat dazed for a few minutes before my sister's wailing swiftly brought tears to my own eyes, which then ran unheedingly down my face. I have always been a silent crier, but all of a sudden this larger-than-life figure's death brought out gut-wrenching sobs from the depth of my soul.

Grief is a personal emotion, and it will manifest itself in the way the griever feels.

My gift to you: No one should tell you how to grieve. Grief is personal, and you can cry if you want to. Sob if you need to get your pent-up emotions out. Go to the cemetery if that is what makes you feel close to your loved one. Do what it takes to mourn your loss. There is nothing wrong with all I have suggested but as you grieve, remember to also think about honoring the person you are mourning. It cannot be a loving grief that is detrimental to you. Your loved one would not appreciate that showing of love if you are slowly killing yourself. Your deceased loved one wants you well and whole. In your grief, never forget to honor your loved one by taking care of yourself. Your greatest show of love is to show love to yourself.

That, my friend, is your gift for today.

Lessons Learned From the School of Hard Knocks

Living this long
Means having gone through life, but
Sometimes life goes through us.
Living is not living
When we do not learn.
What exactly are we learning?
How to live?
Most certainly how to die.
If not how,
Then certainly that there is death.
Living for a number of years,
Almost half a century but undergoing life
Whether in the city or countryside.
We see dead birds, squirrels, cats, and dogs
Run over and crushed and decaying.
Life touches us even when
Our blinders are on.
Life lessons precede us
Even when we deafen our ears,
When we refuse to feel,
Life forces us to look.
Life becomes a living being.
It walks like a giant among us.

Life lives in us,
Regulating us like a traffic light.
We get sick;
Life says slow down.
Life walks tall.
It moves haughtily,
Looking down on us
Disdainfully, knowingly,
Knowing that it is just a matter of time.
Living this long
Through the hurt, pain, and sadness,
Life walks among us,
Teaching us to number our days,
Showing us, who refuse to learn.
Life teaches strong lessons:
How to live with self and others.
How to live while preparing to die.
Life is the principal
In this school of hard knocks
This school called life.

Unwrapping the Gift

Strength for Today

We who are strong have an obligation to bear
with the failings of the weak, and not to please

ourselves. Let each of us please his neighbor for his good, to build him up.

~ Romans 15:1–2

My brother Benji and I were talking about the world and the realities of life. We discussed how certain things that have happened have changed who we are and how we continue to live afterwards. We shared incidents of how some people learned from what happened and others decided they needed more lessons from the school of hard knocks before they learned. We shared stories of people we know who should have learned from devastating situations, but they needed more devastation before they came to terms with the lesson they should have learned already. We even talked about our own family and how certain circumstances should have brought us closer as a family and made us see the light of what life revealed, but while some of us saw the blinding light, others had to have eye surgery to remove the cataracts of indifference to finally see through more life lessons.

The lessons of this life that we experience through just living are not meant to harm us but to teach us valuable lessons. God created us for a purpose, and if we are within his ultimate will, we will see his purpose for us.

I believe that I was born for a purpose. God placed me in the Kroma family. I was taught love, shown love, and told that I was not better than the less fortunate. My parents taught me to love my fellow man; they taught me to treat others like I want to be treated. My parents did a phenomenal job! I am proud of the woman they raised.

I am humble, and I love my fellow man. I am grateful to Martin and Matilda Kroma, the parents God gifted to me as well as gifted me to them. The lessons learned helped to shape the woman I am today. At times I have felt that my upbringing was a weakness because I feel a lot and care for many, and at times I think those attributes worked against me, but those are all what make me the woman that I am.

My gift to you: Are you one of those people who refuses to learn from life? Everything that occurs on our journey through life is a lesson to be learned, a mistake not to be repeated. When we learn from our lessons, we become better, and we become better people. When we do not learn, we tend to repeat or recycle the mistakes we should be correcting in our lives.

As we live our lives, let us use the lessons to improve our lives. We are all born with purpose. Your birth is not an accident of sperm invading egg. Your birth is a divine introduction to the world that you have arrived to fulfill the master plan. Claim your place in this grand scheme of unveiling and proudly take your place. You are here because God has a plan that you will help to fulfill. When we do not learn from life's lessons, then we are sure to receive deeper scars from the wounds of hard knocks. Learn to use life's lessons to your benefit.

That, my friend, is your gift for today.

The Lone Voice

Someone once said,
"Silence is golden."
All my life I have been surrounded by people;
The family I love so much,
A house filled with
Children of different personalities,
Diligent parents who ensured
We all walked the straight line
With integrity.
We have walked that line
Leaning heavily on each other,
Trusting solely on the Lord
Our parents introduced us to.
Now we have cultivated a relationship.
He helps us continue to walk the line
Through all of this though there
Has been the voice of the market,
Those noises trying to derail us,
Trying to show us a different road:
Paths different than the one
Our parents taught us were the right ones.
We stumble and a few times we fall.
Still, we rise, and with one foot in front of the other
We get back up,
Dust off our bottoms, and move forward.

Keep on trudging;
That is what we say to ourselves.
We still hear the noise
From the marketplace called life.
As time has progressed,
We have learned to shut them out,
Out of the corridors of our minds and hearts.
Their silence reigns.
Silence is golden.
We keep walking
Led by the lone voice,
A still, small voice.
The marketplace voices are now dim,
As if miles away,
Even though they too walk beside us,
Constantly chatting like a magpie, whispering,
Telling us that the direction of our walk is pointless.
Still, we walk on,
For deep inside us resides the Lone Voice,
The Comforter who guides,
Constantly whispering
You are on the right track…keep going.
We keep walking
Side by side,
Inspired by the Lone Voice,
This Lone Cheerleader.
We walk and ask the Voice for direction.
We often stop for further instructions.
We wait in silence, sometimes impatiently,
For the only Voice we know will not lead astray,
The Voice that continues to guide and lead

To the final destination,
Our home rejoicing,
A place of peace and rest,
Free from the marketplace,
Home at last, and one with the Lone Voice.

Unwrapping the Gift

Strength for Today

Complete my joy by being of the same mind, having the same love, being in full accord and of one mind.

~ Philippians 2:2

I was raised by conservative parents who had a Christian worldview about life, and my parents raised all of their children as Christians, instilling biblical principles. Over the years, we have all grown closer to God or gone our way into the world with our own convictions. One thing holds dear, though; every one of my siblings wants to be treated fairly, and so do you.

I have been in situations where I was looked over and someone else that I thought less talented was selected. I have been in situations where others were given the prize because their friends were choosing who would win next. I have seen people of other races cross the street when walking towards me, only to cross over again after they pass me by. I have had people look at me and disregard me but then only when someone refers to me as Dr. Ellis do I see respect or interest because of a title.

Each morning the pledge of allegiance is recited at my school, and often I will have a student who is reluctant to stand. I always tell the story of how I have seen students in Sierra Leone going to school with their chairs on their heads so they can sit in class. I encourage students to show respect for our country. They are not required to recite the pledge, but I do encourage them to stand in respect. I must also include that because of religious reasons, I also let students know that they can wait outside and come in after the pledge if they have religious convictions about not standing.

My gift to you: Even though sometimes the odds might seem piled up against you, you cannot lose hope and you cannot keep silent. Speaking up is one way for the oppressor to know that you see them, and you will speak up against unfairness and for your beliefs. Always work to the best of your ability.

That, my friend, is your gift for today.

Looking Forward

I was scared out of my mind,
Did not know what to do
But I prayed.
I could not see past
The mist of uncertainty.
I wanted to know
What was beyond the bend.
All I could do
Was to pray.
Confused.
Previously, the way was always clear.
I could see the potholes and cracks.
Now I had to trust.
Silently, I slid to the ground
And prayed.
I felt a hand
Stretch out towards me,
Asking me to take hold.
I did.
My faith was shaken.
I held on tightly
To the unseen hand
And I kept on praying.
I held on tightly,
Still held on tight.

I kept looking down,
Depending on my human vision
Which I already knew
Was faulty and fleeting.
One hand gripped mine,
The other gently tilted my chin
Upwards.
I heard his whisper,
Look up to me.
Keep your eyes fixed
Firmly and only on me.
I am your help
In all times
Whether joyous or in trouble.
I looked upward.
I kept my gaze heavenward,
I keep praying,
Keeping the lines of communication
Open.
I felt his love
Surround me.
I kept my gaze trained
Only on him—
Then I found the peace.
Sweet, perfect peace.

Unwrapping the Gift

Strength for Today

Therefore encourage one another and build one another up, just as you are doing.

~ 1 Thessalonians 5:11

I now understand what it means to "speak life" into oneself. Despite the naysayers, you must speak positivity to yourself and give yourself a blood transfusion. No one can make you feel inferior without your consent (Eleanor Roosevelt). Think about that! Wake up each day with intention. Today, I am going to feel better about myself. Today, I will not wallow in self-pity about what happened to me. Today, I will stop making excuses. Today... Today... Today...

You must wake up each day with an intention. You must live intentionally.

I intend to focus on what I have. I intend to have a grateful heart. I intend to love. I intend to forgive and not allow anyone to live rent-free in my head. I intend to do what I say I intend to do. I might struggle, but I will do my best to stay intentional until it becomes second nature to me.

Secondly, you must speak life into yourself. Each morning or whenever you awake, look yourself in the mirror and say, "I am capable. I am enough. I am beautiful. I am handsome. I can do this [whatever "this" means], and most importantly, believe it! Why speak life and positivity into yourself if you do not believe your own words? Let us be realistic. Maybe, in the beginning, you struggle to believe but as time goes on and you gain confidence and your voice becomes stronger; you will start to believe your own words.

Practice does make better. If you practice negativity, then negativity is what you will get good at. On the other hand, when you practice positivity, positivity is what you will get better at. Remember, I am talking about you and not about depending on someone else to be positive to you. Speak life into yourself.

Now there is another catalyst: the voices in your head that you have allowed to live rent-free, the voices that have told you,

- You will never amount to anything.
- You are ugly.
- You know you cannot accomplish that
- Look at yourself. You are crazy to even think someone like you could ever get out of this neighborhood or this way of life.
- You think talking 'white' will get you out of this neighborhood?
- You are just like the rest of us.
- Why are you talking like white people?
- You will always be trash.
- You are nothing.
- He cannot love you.

- You are not good enough.
- You are too black.
- You are too white.

The naysayers are envious and jealous. They lie. They lie! Yes, they do, because of their own insecurities. They do not want you to let your light out. They are scared of your light. If your light comes out, it will shine on their darkness and reveal who they really are.

Why are you listening to someone who has never accomplished their own dream? Why are you listening to someone who is scared to death of seeing you rise up out of the ashes of your situation? That does not make sense, does it? It does not. Period. Speak life into yourself.

My gift to you: Each morning when I wake up, I thank God because I acknowledge my blessings. Waking up: I am in a very comfortable bed, got eyes to see (through my glasses), my body is able to move, etc. Do you see why I wake up with positivity? It all starts with gratitude and then, eventually, the things we do not have will take up less of our thoughts because we become focused on what we do have.

Fast-forward: I am just about to walk out the door. Now, this is when the magic happens. I have a full-length mirror in my garage, and as I walk out, that is when I look at my full image and talk to the woman in the mirror. I say to her, "Girl, you look good! Now go show the world the God in you." My God-given power unfurls as I strut out and into my car to start a day propelled by God's guidance and the spirit of positivity.

Take note, people, and try it. Do not discard this advice until you have tried it at least three times.

Practice makes permanent!

That, my friend, is your gift for today.

Never Give Up

Tried to acclimatize
To my environment
Even though it was different.
My stamina is gone
Living in this solar place.
Oxygen is long displaced,
Sucked out of the tiny pores,
Always aspiring to see
The people working
On so grand a scale.
They work so there is no useless living.
They work tirelessly,
With great precaution.
This altitude we have climbed
Will not fade away.
We will keep on working,
Keep fighting;
Our goals and dreams
One day will be realized.
This work is not in vain.

Unwrapping the Gift

Strength for Today

These things I have spoken to you, that in me you may have peace. In the world you will have trib-ulation; but be of good cheer, I have overcome the world.

~ John 16:33

When I was a teenager, I heard a pastor tell this story. There was a man who had an ongoing battle with Satan. Each day, the issues surrounding his life seemed insurmountable, and he was discouraged and despondent. Satan was destroying all that he had worked so hard to obtain.

One day, the man was passing by a church, and he was drawn to it. He entered and took a seat. The pastor preached a soul-stirring sermon that pricked the man's heart, and he ran forward to accept Jesus Christ as his personal Lord and Savior. The man was overcome with joy, and he rejoiced and went on home, telling everyone who would listen about what the Lord had done for him.

The man started living his life the Christian way, and he soon noticed that Satan was not battling him any longer, and in his relief, he relaxed and began to enjoy his blessings like he was before his battles with Satan began.

One day while he was relaxed in his kitchen, Satan appeared and began to wrestle with him. As Satan overpowered him and threw him to the ground, the man cried out to God for help and Satan left him and went into other rooms of his home to destroy them. The man was relieved but disappointed that even though God helped him and Satan did not destroy his kitchen, he still destroyed the other parts of his home.

A few nights later, Satan appeared while the man was in his restroom and began to battle with him again. The man cried out to God and the Lord came to his rescue and Satan immediately went to the other parts of the home to destroy everything in his path but the restroom where the man remained untouched and safe with God.

The man was appalled when he saw the destruction of the other parts of his home. He screamed at God, "Why are you not protecting me and my home like you promised the day I accepted you as Lord and Savior? Look at the state and condition of my house!"

God smiled, and took the man's hand. "My son, you accepted me, but you have only allowed me space in a few parts of your life. You have still maintained control over most of it. So I am not in control of the places you still hold firmly in your grasp. You accepted me, but you have not relinquished full control to me. Give me everything and see how your life will change."

The man fell to his knees and asked God to forgive him because he realized that indeed, he had not given God total control of his life. The man repented and handed his life and all he had to God.

A few nights later, Satan reappeared to the man while the man sat at his dining room table, Satan started to put his hands up to strike a blow as he advanced towards the man. Satan saw God, and he ran out of the room and into other sections of the man's home to destroy them. Every room Satan ran through to try to destroy, God was there, and not a single part of his home was destroyed.

My gift to you: You cannot give some of your life to God and expect full coverage. When we totally hand our lives to God, he takes care of us. When things go bad, we can totally rely on God to see us through. When our family members die, we expect that we will see them again in heaven, so we have hope. When we lose our jobs, we know he will provide. When our friends forsake us, we know he is a friend that will stick closer than a brother. When we hand ourselves totally and completely to God, trouble will come, but we know that God will see us through.

If you are reading carefully, you will see that I am not promising you the lack of trouble. However, what I can assure you of is that God will see you through when you put your life fully in his care. Hand your life totally and completely to God and see the total transformation and peace you will receive.

That, my friend, is your final gift for today.

The Gift

A Glimpse through the Window of My Soul

A Glimpse Through the Window of My Soul invites everyone to catch a glimpse of who I am through the lenses of my thoughts in poetry. Each poem is written at all hours as I experienced situations or reflected on the past and is an exact expression of my feelings and thoughts about the given subjects. Each section characterizes how I feel about hope, love, the past, blessings, provision, and family, and my love is poured out to you through the ultimate gift of giving advice. The intent of The Gift is not to cure any ailment, but the overwhelming goal for all who read these thoughts that have been wrenched from my soul is to bring comfort from your turmoil into hope everlasting, as it did for me. I have found peace that transcends all comprehension, and I present you with that gift.

Blessings now and always,

E. E. E.

I have told you these things, so that in me you may have peace. In this world you will have trouble. But take heart! I have overcome the world.

~ John 3:33

This is an amazing book, and the title is very apt;
it truly is a gift!
Editor Lee Ann at FirstEditing.com

CPSIA information can be obtained
at www.ICGtesting.com
Printed in the USA
BVHW031155311022
650744BV00012B/447

9 781662 849695